CW01239106

John Bosley is retired and therefore thoroughly enjoying life. With his wife, Kate, he is currently joint president of the San Fairy Ann Cycling Club, based in Kent. John has lived in Maidstone for over 30 years and is very proud of his four adult children—Charlotte, Hannah, Josh and Sarah—and at the moment three grandchildren—Rudy, Bailey and Wren.

John has written this book as a humorous and informative record of an amazing tandem cycle 'round France in summer 2023 so that he can remember it. It is hard enough trying to remember what you did the day before on a cycle tour, let alone 74 days of cycling!

To Kate, because she's the best and was an equal part in this adventure.

To family and friends and also to the snails around France, Facebook followers, many of whom seem to have become friends.

John Bosley

SNAILS AROUND FRANCE

A Tandem Bike Ride All the Way
Around France

AUSTIN MACAULEY PUBLISHERS
LONDON * CAMBRIDGE * NEW YORK * SHARJAH

Copyright © John Bosley 2024

The right of John Bosley to be identified as author of this work has been asserted by the author in accordance with sections 77 and 78 of the Copyright, Designs and Patents Act 1988.

All rights reserved. No part of this publication may be reproduced, stored in a retrieval system, or transmitted in any form or by any means, electronic, mechanical, photocopying, recording, or otherwise, without the prior permission of the publishers.

Any person who commits any unauthorised act in relation to this publication may be liable to criminal prosecution and civil claims for damages.

The story, experiences, and words are the author's alone.

A CIP catalogue record for this title is available from the British Library.

ISBN 9781035860128 (Paperback)
ISBN 9781035860135 (Hardback)
ISBN 9781035860142 (ePub e-book)

www.austinmacauley.com

First Published 2024
Austin Macauley Publishers Ltd®
1 Canada Square
Canary Wharf
London
E14 5AA

Kate Bosley, Alison Millar, David Butterworth, Justine and Stuart Henderson, and the authors of other books whose thoughts and ideas are scattered through this book in order to make it sound authoritative (they are acknowledged in the bibliography).

Table of Contents

Introduction	11
Prologue	12
Planning	18
The Route	19
The Tour de France	23
Luggage (Panniers)	24
How (and How Not) to Prepare for and Ride a Multi-Day Event	26
Mountain Climbs	28
Riding Today and Tomorrow (After Yesterday)	29
Wait to Eat/Drink Until You Feel Hungry/Thirsty at Your Peril	34
Not Testing Out Your Kit and Bike Before the Event	33
Not Checking the Weather Forecast	34
The Bike	40
Applying for a Visa	42
The Stoker	48
The Journey Ready? Go!	50
Bibliography	189

Introduction

"No, I'm sorry. We'll be away then doing our cycle around France, and then I'll start writing the book."

"That sounds lovely. What's your book about?" (I stared blankly.)

It may not have been such a silly question. (Putting aside the *lovely* comment suggested they had absolutely no idea about what the challenge entailed. They did not listen to what I said.) I could have been facetious and said it's about the variety of edible snails found in France. Friends and the infinite more non-friends will know that's exactly what I said.

That partly explains the name of the book, but more importantly, it describes our pace-setting strategy—to think of the bigger picture and ride comfortably, within ourselves. The rest, as they say, is exactly what it says on the tin.

The problem, though, is knowing what a reader wants to read. Beauty, of course, is in the eye of the beholder, which doesn't help as we all want something different from the same thing. Some people want to know about the bike (typically tedious types); others actually have less of an interest in cycling and want to know about the local history, geography, and red-light districts. If someone is desperate to discover themselves, they may be interested in planning and preparation. Yet there are those who, despite advice, embark on their unnecessarily challenging rides from Madagascar to Siberia, often hitching rides on the backs of lorries and shipping containers. Typically, they then write a book, showcasing everyone what an idiot they are.

This book will attempt to do all these things and more, in blatant disregard of any sales targets (there aren't any.) Also, if you want to read some more, head to Facebook and 'Snails around France' to find photos, videos, and additional tours we have undertaken.

"Do the different varieties have different tastes?"

"Good question; I'll have to try each of them to find out. Perhaps put them in a snail race and eat the winner first," she looked a bit shocked.

I've crossed that invisible line again.

"No, only joking; it would be the loser, of course."

Prologue

If something can go wrong, it will.

Kate and I were cycling on our tandem over a few days from Hexham in Northumberland to Chichester, West Sussex, with Simon, the partner of one of our daughters (Hannah, I think), in May 2022. Heading to Sheffield, we had booked a room for Kate and me and a twin room for Simon and David, a friend of mine (allegedly), in the Holiday Inn Express (they still haven't forgiven me for the occasion that I booked them a double room.) David tested positive for COVID the night before our trip began and couldn't join us on account of us not letting him. We were also meeting a cycling friend, Clare, who had booked her own room in the hotel next door to join us for the remainder of the ride. To save money, it made sense for Simon and me to share a room, cancel the double room, and Kate would stay with Clare.

    We arrived in Sheffield rather late that day. (Who would want to arrive early in Sheffield?) Clare had messaged to say she was enjoying a (bottle or two of) wine from her hotel bar. We arrived on our tandem with Simon on his bike and pulled over in front of our hotel, about 2 hours later than expected due to mechanicals and punctures. Just across the way, we could see a hotel next door, which was a Crowne Plaza. We cycled around the back of our hotel, under some arches, and along the road to drop Kate off at the Crowne Plaza with her pannier bag. When we got there, the hotel was up above us, on higher ground, so we cycled around looking for a way in, then over some footbridges, and eventually ended up back at our hotel. When you are touring, it often seems that at the end of the day, when you think that you've reached your destination, these problems arise. It was then we realised that the arches we had cycled under supported a driveway up to Kate and Clare's hotel. Beginning to get even later and in need of food, we quickly cycled up the driveway, dropping Kate off at the entrance. Although Kate is visually impaired and did not have her white stick with her or guide dog (obviously), we knew that Clare was already there (that's my excuse.) With relief, Simon and I cycled back around to the entrance of our hotel. The doors, however, would not open. To the side, some doors were open, but into a meeting or conference that we felt reluctant to interrupt. We spent about 15 minutes trying every door in the place when a man came out to speak to us.

"Hello, can I help you?"

"Yes, please; we can't see how to get into the hotel."

"No one is staying in this hotel."

"But we have a reservation."

"No one is staying here. You are staying there," he said, pointing at the Crowne Plaza.

"I have a reservation here."

"No one is staying here; everyone is staying over there."

"Oh, I see, we have all been moved into the Crowne Plaza!" What a waste of time! We had spent all that time and now had to go back to where we had abandoned Kate. Still, Simon and I laughed; at least we were all going to be in the same place. Finally, we could get settled, have a shower, and go out for some food. As we cycled back up the driveway, Kate was walking down the path, looking hot and bothered with her bag and without her white stick or her guide dog (not that I actually noticed at that moment.)

"I can't believe it, after all that we are in the Crowne Plaza with you!"

"I can't believe it, after all that I'm in the Best Western across the road."

"What?"

Kate grabbed her white stick off the tandem whilst quickly explaining what had happened to her. Having been dropped off with her pannier by an uncaring husband (what a bastard), she went into reception and explained that a friend she was sharing a room with was expecting her. She was asked the name of the friend but could only recall her first name, 'Clare'. Clare recently reverted to using her maiden name, so Kate had to find her on social media whilst explaining that she was visually impaired and apologising for her slowness. Having found the name, the receptionist was sorry to inform Kate that there was no one by that name. Kate corrected her, explained that she was upstairs, and gave her a call, "CLARE!" (No, a phone call); Oh right, "Hi Clare, sorry, but they don't have your name on the system—or I've got it wrong! I'm in reception."

"No problem, I'll come down to get you."

After a few minutes, Kate called Clare again, "Hi, how are you doing?"

"I'm waiting in reception for you."

"I'm in reception—I can't see you." (Well, she is visually impaired.)

"Kate, which hotel are you in? You know I'm in the Best Western, don't you?"

Kate looked up at the receptionist, who just guessed, "Wrong hotel?"

I am tempted to comment that they offered no support to a visually impaired person to safely relocate—but as the husband, I was no better as I had cycled past and, in disbelief, offered equally non-existent support!

Simon and I arrived at the reception, where I said hello to the receptionist and explained that she had probably just met my wife.

"Yes, I hope she is okay and in the correct hotel now."

"Yes, I hope so too," I laughed. Her expression suggested she was a little confused by my comment, so after an embarrassing pause, "Anyhow, we'd like to check-in, please."

"Oh, are you staying here then?" (Bite your tongue, John.)

"Yes, the name's Bosley…John Bosley." I honestly think that is the first time I've used that line. If you know, you know, and if you are younger than about 55, you have little chance of knowing what I'm referring to—just Google it!

"Bosley John Bosley, I'm sorry, no one of that name has a room reserved."

A moment lapsed during which I wanted to swear rather loudly and publicly, but for once I didn't.

"Well, we were booked in the Holiday Inn next door, but we have been told that guests have moved here. Wait a minute, could the booking be under the name of David Butterworth? He was due to come, but has COVID."

"That'll do it."

What a relief when she confirmed the reservation.

"When we booked, we were advised we could keep our bikes in our room. I assume we are on the ground floor?"

Of course not. That would have been far too easy. We were on the third floor, but they were able to find us a conference room to put the bikes in and code our key cards; they opened our room and also gave us access to the bikes in the morning. Getting somewhere at last!

The time was now about 7 p.m. so we quickly headed for our room and showers. Kate confirmed she was safe with Clare. They had booked a table for 7.30 at a pub next to the hotel. I said we'd be there as soon as possible. The next message said, "We are here. Inside, with wine and pork scratchings."

"Just about to leave—give us 3 hours to find it!"

Not very funny. By 8 p.m., Simon and I had arrived at the agreed location, and they were nowhere to be seen. I then had a silly conversation with two female bartenders.

"Hi, we are meeting a couple of women here; lucky us! One is visually impaired; have you served them?"

"Not that I recall."

"They said they were drinking wine and eating pork scratchings."

"We do serve wine and pork scratchings. Shirley, have you served someone pork scratchings?"

"What, tonight?"

"Tonight?" She checked with me.

"Yes, we are not yet a day late." (Any 'edge' was not intended. It is always strange when you say something light-hearted that you hear doesn't sound that way. Do you let the moment go or apologise and explain it was a joke?)

"Yes, tonight, Shirley."

"Ooh, I think I did, but I can't remember who."

I decided I was wasting their time. "It's okay, we'll have another look for them. Sorry to bother you."

We continued our search and found Kate and Clare in the restaurant next door. Clare thought it was part of the pub—talk about the blind leading the blind! We had a lovely, filling meal and an extra pint to help de-stress. What a relief that all this is now over.

The next morning, when we went to retrieve our bikes, the key fob didn't work on the conference room door. We should have expected that, really. We tried the door, and it opened because people were inside, and a conference was about to start. Simon's bike was missing, and the perplexed recumbents—sorry, incumbents—were just considering what to do with the tandem. This time, at least, it was all fairly quickly sorted, and we got on our way.

When things do go wrong, they can make great stories (retrospectively). That event happened on a 5-day tour—what stories would a 3-month tour have?

Riding a tandem (is the answer).

But what is the question, perhaps:

How do I include my partner in my cycling obsession? Or how do I ride with my partner without constantly being left behind? Better still, what's the easiest way to get a divorce?

Kate and I have a number of reasons for riding a tandem and some key thoughts on making it work. So why do we ride a tandem?

a. Kate had a serious cycling accident and can no longer ride solo. Riding a tandem means that I can continue to ride guilt-free, and Kate can continue to ride.
b. In our 10th year of tandem riding, it has become the norm. We both just feel like we have been out on a bike ride.

How do you make it work?

1. Dispense with any sense of self-ego.
2. Same as 1.

With regards to the first point, and in many ways also the second, one of the hardest mind games is when your ego is telling you the other person is not trying hard enough, if at all. If you are riding a solo bike, there will be times when you find it hard, but there is no one to blame. So why blame someone when in tandem? A. A. Milne described this very well whilst riding his tandem trike with his brother Ken. This was at the advent of cycling in the late 1800s as young children.

Their tandem was a trike, and the pilot (his brother) sat at the rear in charge of steering and coming to a stop. (Which also includes the speed you choose to go downhill—a possible point of conflict, especially if you are at the front and have no control.) Milne was well aware that when he was at the high point of effort, bent over his front wheel, panting, sweating, and gritting his teeth, he would become increasingly convinced, at every pedal revolution, that his brother had his feet up and was enjoying the increasingly spectacular views. He did surrender that his brother was possibly looking at him and thinking he was putting on an act and pretending that he was making an effort. (It's Too Late Now, 1939)

To my knowledge, Kate and I have no such concerns. We are either typically putting in the effort of a similar measure, or at any given time, one of us may be helping out the other, but we are both getting there, and compromise by either of us is a part of teamwork. We certainly did not complete Simon Warren's 100 hill climbs with just one of us doing the work (and if we did, one of us is bloody brilliant.) Now, if Kate has a different view, then I am shocked and deluded, and she is a bitch. As is life.

I know, thank you.

Planning

If you have the time, planning can be quite enjoyable. Some, admittedly not many, would say it was as fun as the ride itself. I've heard people say you can experience a journey three times when you plan it, live it, and then remember it. However, the planning part also has the potential to raise your levels of anxiety. The things that worried me were:

1. Being able to find adequate sustenance each day (fluid and about 3-5,000 calories.)
2. Being able to reach our destination each day (will weather, illness, accident, or mechanicals be a barrier?).
3. Would any of the routes turn out to be dangerous due to heavy traffic and poor cycling infrastructure?
4. Would our visa come through in time?

Things that could be a worry, but I did not lose any sleep over were cost; would we be fit enough? Would the accommodation let us down? And criminals (though I think we were actually leaving them behind in the UK; we call them politicians these days.)

The Route

I guess before going into too much detail, a legitimate question might be why? We love cycling, of course, and we love it most when we are on tour. It involves reaching a destination (one hopes), and it's a bit of a challenge! We hoped that we'd remain fit enough until I retired so that we could use the flexibility of time to tackle a significant challenge. As I mentioned, we had already completed Simon Warren's 100 Greatest Hill Climbs and were the first tandem riders to do so. Now on to something different. Kate had read a book by Anna Hughes, 'Eat, Sleep, Cycle; A Bike Ride around the Coast of Britain'. It seemed like the sort of challenge we'd enjoy, so Kate suggested a similar plan around France. Although the thought of attempting to stick as close to the border across the Pyrenees and then again through the Alps briefly cast some doubt in my mind, I decided to put that aside and began to scope out the practicalities.

Firstly, how far is that? My initial, "Hey Google, how far is it 'round France?" didn't work, but I have planned many cycle routes using Garmin's cycle mapping software—from home (Maidstone, England) to Bordeaux; John O'Groats to Land's End to Margate; Malin Head to Mizen Head across Ireland, all successfully. I thought for an hour plotting a rough route would give me some insight—it did. Firstly, I got the insight that the software couldn't cope with the whole circumnavigation of France on one route. I did manage to get from Calais to Biriatou on what I named the France Western Border segment (in case you are eager to know, 2,462 kilometres with 15,603 metres of climbing. I hadn't even plotted across mountains yet.) It took about 3 hours of plotting. Did I think to myself, okay, this isn't going to work, no. Why not? Is that laziness or perseverance—are they part of the same thing? This way of mapping for this specific task had to be a waste of time, but no, I just carried on night after night for a week, creating each segment. The next segment (France Southern Border) was from Biriatou to Ceret (almost across to the Med) before the software couldn't cope (only 977.87 kilometres, but wait for it…over 25,000 metres of climbing!). By the end of the week, I had created 6 segments plotting a rough guide around France, totalling 6,523 kilometres with 74,675 metres of climbing. What did I learn? Absolutely sod all, though it had raised a few questions.

Those routes through the Pyrenees—were they okay for road bikes?

Would there ever be places to stay in such remote locations as Defile de Tournont (I googled that and it came up with 'Missing students found dead in Pyrenees'.) or Col Cap de Long (I googled that, and a website, 'The Col Collective' ominously warns that 'In the French Pyrenees lies the Lac de Cap-de-Long, a climb that few cyclists will know but, once tackled, few will ever forget'.)?

Is it futile (more importantly, demoralising) to go along a road that we'll have to come back down just to go near a border?

Is going into another country, because the road goes that way, creating unnecessary mileage (Le Tour de France does!).

Hmmm, with regards to the perimeter, some parameters are needed.

My first thoughts were:

1. Perhaps no crossing borders—that might make things simpler or more manageable.
2. No point in going down dead ends, roads that just lead to endless one-way loops, or roads that only cross a border.
3. Roads should be safe and not gravelly or broken—this is road cycling; certainly they should not be like the Strade Bianche (white gravel roads) in Italy—yes, we have done some. Yes, it was an experience. No, not ever again (sometimes a double negative does serve to emphasise a point whilst allowing for a change of heart). And unlike the 3-lane A14 dual carriageway that bypasses Newmarket in England. (Yes, we have time-trialled on that a few times!)
4. Err, hold on! I wonder what other cyclists have come up with—perhaps a standard exists!

First stop, that 'Eat, Sleep, Cycle' book—what did Anna have to say? "…following the river from London until it became the sea, then following the sea for 4,000 miles…" That could get confusing when the sea is not in sight.

Second stop, Anna isn't the only one to have done it; what did Mike Carter's 'One man and his bike' have to say? "…all I had to do was keep…the sea on my right." That's it? And if there is no sea to see, Mike?

The third stop has to be Google. "Hey Google, what are the rules for cycle touring?"

Mrs Google answered, "The website Cyclescope.net has 30 rules for bicycle touring; would you like to hear them?"

"Yes, you sexy beast you!" (Does anyone else engage in casual talk with Alexa or Google? No, oh.)

28 of the 30 rules do not offer any advice about route choice, but the 7th Rule advises, "Don't plan too much; always go with the mood and the spirit of the place." I like that. The 8th rule says, "If your visa is too short to ride it all without missing all the beauty, get a lift or take a train." So, one of the rules of cycle touring is not to cycle!

I did also pose a provocative question on a bicycle travellers Facebook page that went along the lines of, "What rules do travellers set for themselves when setting a touring challenge, or is 'cheating' acceptable?"

For most, the question did not go down well. But to keep it short, the answers fell into two camps. The small camp wanted a challenge such as at least 100 miles a day and no lifts, unless essential, and if so, go back to where you were picked up so that there are no gaps in the journey. And the large camps (ironically, those unlikely to stay in a large holiday camp) who take it as it comes and chill. Also ironically, this large camp had a significant percentage of highly stressed people who vehemently argued that the question was stupid and that there should be no 'rules' and I should certainly avoid the word 'challenge' (so, at least two rules of their own already).

"Your comfort zone is the mental equivalent of an easy ride. It's pleasant enough and might have some sticky bits where the road ramps up or you feel a little bit tired, but it's well within your capability," says Kyle Macrae, author of The Mental Cyclist. "Your Mental Cyclist Challenge should be something that does set your heart on fire. Something that motivates you to push beyond your comfort zone. Something that makes you think you might fail (you won't.) It's something you'd really, really love to do. You will."

My 3 rules—staying within the French border, not cycling down roads that require a return journey or one-way systems, and not cycling on gravelly or dangerous roads—began to look as good as anything for planning daily routes. It's a pity I hadn't thought of this before wasting time on that Garmin mapping exercise!

I did add a fourth clause to give a nod in the direction of the chilled but stressed touring majority: if I feel like it, plot the route that I was going to enjoy and ignore rules 1, 2, and 5 (I was taught and learnt to read the questions before starting the exam! Well, apart from that time, I forgot to look carefully in the envelope for the second sheet of questions, finished and left the exam room before anyone else, feeling very pleased with myself, and I got an 'F'! That was the end of my photography career.)

The Tour de France

If you are a road cyclist, this part may be unnecessary, but for anyone else, it provides context to one or two stories that are told on our Tour de France. Don't worry, as I am the author, it'll be simple!

Le Tour is a multi-stage cycle race. That means it takes place over multiple days, with a race (a stage) each day. It's 21 stages long (so 21 racing days.) Each stage is like a single race with a winner for that day (the stage winner), but the cyclist whose overall time across all the stages is fastest is the overall winner (by the way, the cyclist that is leading the overall race at the end of each stage gets to wear the yellow jersey, the 'Maillot Jaune'.)

It's for top professional teams; you can't just enter it like the London Marathon—and perhaps, surprisingly, it's a team sport.

In the early days of the Tour de France (the first of which was in 1903), the tour really did race right 'round France. Not hugging the border, but none the less typically producing the approximate hexagonal shape of France and travelling very long distances. The first edition of the tour, after the First World War, took place in 1919 (having not taken place since 1914.) But it's a typical example of the nature of the tour at the time. Starting in Paris, the route went out to the coast at Le Havre and then roughly followed the shape of France all the way 'round France to Dunkerque before heading back to Paris (5,560 kilometres).

Luggage (Panniers)

In the prologue, I mentioned dropping Kate off at a hotel with her pannier (singular). Any previous tours we had done were typically over five or six days and had been with one pannier each for cycle kit and evening wear and a third pannier lying across the top of the pannier rack for 'everything else'. Would this suffice for a complete circumnavigation of France in about 12 weeks?

We agreed that we did not want to be struggling over the Alps and the Pyrenees with much more weight than normal. As we were restricting our challenge to France, we convinced ourselves that we would be able to get support or standard spares/parts for the bike when needed, rather than carrying heavy spares. We had often compared what we carried for the two of us in tandem with three medium-size pannier bags with what our friend, David, carried on his bike—three large pannier bags, with a further roll-up bag strapped to the top, a bag perched upon the top tube, and a handlebar bag for knick-knacks (let's call it a handbag.)

Items in our panniers for this trip:

- 2 sets of evening wear,
  (Lightweight and easy to hand wash!)
- 1 pair of cycling socks
  (Double up as evening socks.)
- Leg warmers
- Arm warmers

- Long-sleeve base layer
- 1 cycling jacket
- 1 cycling jersey
- Gloves
- 1 pair of cycle shorts

The extra pannier would hold:

- A packable rain jacket each
- A pair of sandals for Kate
- A pair of aqua shoes for me
- A pair of waterproof overshoes each
- 5 spare inner tubes
- Multi-tool kit
- Chamois cream

- 2 spare tyres
- Gold-secure D lock
- Tandem cables
- Pregnancy test kit
- Spare disc brake pads
- Spare disc
- Spare chain

Germolene/Sudocrem
Toothbrushes and toothpaste
Medicines
Spare chain rings
Spare carbon belt

Electrics (charging cables in French plug)
Compact electric pump
Lubricant
Emergency sleeping bag/blanket
Straps

Each of us wearing:

Mitts
Helmet and cap
Cycling jacket
Lycra shorts

Socks
Cleated MTB cycle shoes
Cycling Jersey (possibly an extra layer or two for Kate!)

So, what would David be carrying, in addition to our kit:

A pair of shoes
Waterproof trousers
Waterproof helmet cover (like a shower cap…in fact…a shower cap.)
Macadamia Nuts
Tooth pics
David's special clothes hanger
Face masks
Swimming trunks
Jelly babies
Shirt
T-shirt
Winter gloves
Cycling over trousers
Waterproof coat

Bars
Gels
Foil and grease-proof paper
Sweatshirt
First aid kit
Bungie
Baby wipes
Zip ties
Plastic carrier bag (from 1997)
Deodorant
Anti-bac hand gel
Mints
Pump (in addition to his own compact electric pump)
A cuddly toy and a cabbage

(By the way, the pregnancy test kit was a joke. It got damp and indicated I was either pregnant or had COVID.)

Our luggage weighed less than 20kg in total; you would think we had a flight to catch!

How (and How Not) to Prepare for and Ride a Multi-Day Event

Pacing

For some, it is tempting to go too hard and use up too much energy from the start. We did an amazing ride around Scotland in 2019 with our friends David and Simon (this was the occasion I booked them a double room.) It was Simon's first multi-day event, and he was looking forward to the challenge, perhaps worrying it might not be challenging enough: The North Coast 500 (well worth doing despite the risk of drowning.) He suggested that he ride in front and sustain a steady 20mph to begin with so we could tuck in behind. David has a similar approach to hill climbs; attack them from the get-go and carry the speed through to the top—or should I say, stop about halfway up and stand over your handlebars, breathing like a donkey and sweating like a pig (he's not vegetarian.) This isn't to say that our approach is perfect—we are probably far too cautious, fearing we may not get to the top, just travelling at a snail's pace on big climbs!

Anyway, by day 2, Simon was proving to be an excellent snail imitator. (To be fair, it was lumpy, quite sharp, humpy, and bumpy.) But the point is that cycling like this is about riding at a sustainable pace, a pace that will allow you to get up and carry on the next day, not overtired and not injured. Of course, it's very tempting to chase down a rider that you can see ahead on a mountain climb, and we all succumb to that! (Don't even mention e-bikes or bikes with a basket on the front or a tandem; the challenge is often presented on a plate, and temptation can be difficult to resist.) So, our pacing challenge was to ride 'within ourselves' much slower and more relaxed than we are accustomed to.

Pacing is also about allowing some time in the day to see the world and perhaps even meet people. This means trying to avoid being like the cyclist who is angry with himself in H.G. Wells' 'The Wheels of Chance':

'There's no hurry, sir, none whatever. I came out for exercise, gentle exercise, and to notice the scenery and to botanize. And no sooner do I get on that accursed machine than off I go hammer and tongs; I never look to right or left, never notice a flower, never see a view—get hot, juicy, red like a grilled chop. Here I am, sir. Come from Guildford in something under the hour. Why, sir?'

Mr Hoopdriver shook his head.

'Because I'm a damned fool, sir. Because I've reservoirs and reservoirs of muscular energy, and one or other of them is always leaking. It's a most interesting road, birds and trees, I've no doubt, and wayside flowers, and there's nothing I should enjoy more than watching them.

But I can't. Get me on that machine, and I have to go. Get me on anything, and I have to go. And I don't want to go a bit. Why should a man rush about like a rocket, all pace and fizzle? Why? It makes me furious. I can assure you, sir, I go scorching along the road, and cursing aloud at myself for doing it.'

(The Wheels of Chance, 1896)

Mountain Climbs

Kate and I don't struggle with the concept of climbing hills; we might occasionally struggle up them, but then they are usually very steep, gravelly, or cobbled! We once skidded on gravel on a 30% incline, stopped, and then had to push the tandem up, and we hated it. So now, we just keep going.

The main reason this book is called Snails Around France is because we very quickly get into low gear on a mountain and then just pedal at a snail's pace all the way up. Climbing mountains is always worthwhile. As cyclists, we are well matched, and that may also help. A. A. Milne, the author of Winnie the Pooh, described something as 'not worthwhile doing' in his autobiography, 'It's Too Late Now'. As a child in the late 1800s, he lived in the village of Limpsfield, which had a steep road climbing up out of the village, Limpsfield Hill (there are no surprises here.) He enjoyed bike riding with his brother Ken and described how they would push their bikes up the road as it was a steep incline and not worth riding up it. But Milne then goes on to tell the story of struggling to ride a tandem trike (with a rear-seated pilot) up Limpsfield Hill with Ken. It should have been worthwhile doing it, as an uncle had offered them sixpence each if they could do it. (A lot of pocket money for two young boys.)

They set off up the hill, zigzagging across the road, puffing and panting. At times, they come to a standstill, with brakes on to stop themselves from rolling backwards and then pushing on again. But they did not dismount; exhausted yet elated, they collapsed on the grassy common at the summit. They basked in the achievement and shared the excitement and anticipation of receiving their reward and how they would spend it. Then they were 'disqualified', and for them, civilisation had ended. Their uncle said that the rule was that you don't stop; everyone knows that (I reckon I could have been that uncle.) Milne does add that he knows many things are not worth doing as soon as you discover that you can't do them! So, can you, or can't you? For now, anyway we can. If we can't, we'll get an E-Tandem or possibly a hover tandem by then (and I fancy some of Marty McFly's self-lacing shoes, please).

Riding Today and Tomorrow (After Yesterday)

Kate and I train at least 5 days a week, often every day. It does sound like a lot, but we have always felt that back-to-back spins, even if they are only for 30 to 45 minutes, get our bodies used to and expect the effort. On a tour, rather than rest days, we would prefer to do shorter, easier distances up to about 70 kilometres. We prioritise this back-to-back training over riding long distances, though we are working much harder for the shorter time, which does seem to compensate. That doesn't exclude regular longer rides, however, but we do feel it's important that you get your bum used to getting back in the saddle the next day, enabling you to cycle if you have tired legs and a lack of energy (though regular rides also help reduce those symptoms.) Kate also runs marathons—you just must pretend not to be impressed and ignore it—and did the virtual London Marathon just a few weeks before we set off. I don't pretend; I'm just not impressed and just ignore this silly behaviour. (Yes, she is visually impaired, so she has some very kind and generous guide runners and does most training on a treadmill.)

It's worth noting that it's possible to set off on a long tour and grow into it day by day…but start off short, slow, and manageable, and allow the body to adjust!

Annually, we would like to get some early season cycling in as part of our training buildup and this year we booked a holiday in Mallorca with a small group of friends: Andy and Lisa, and Dom and Sarah. Though Sarah is far too sensible and enjoys a relaxing holiday whilst we go 'hell for leather' on our bikes, she will likely live the longest out of us.

Andy, well, he's probably not a cyclist at all. He turns up because Lisa does, sort of like her bodyguard. He only cycles on these holidays and fits in a bit of training just a few weeks before. The thing is, he still manages to keep the rest of us in his sights. We don't encourage him to take it too seriously.

Lisa, well, she's just a nutter. She is a good cyclist and can ride extremes of cycling, but other things, like breaking the ice on Lake Windermere to go for a swim in winter, deserve no admiration whatsoever. In the past, women like this were put in mental institutions, and quite rightly so. Kate and Lisa would almost definitely be witches because of their bizarre behaviours.

And then there's Dom. The main problem with Dom is his sense of humour, which makes him quite challenging to get along with, mainly because it's like mine. The great things about Dom are still to be discovered.

It was a great ten days away, with perfect weather, great cycling, and plenty of food and drink. The island recognises the benefits to its economy by meeting the needs of cyclists; consequently, cyclists flood the island in spring. But as well as great cycling, we changed a few of our ideas for the tour.

On one particularly challenging day, we cycled about 45 kilometres to meet up with some cycling friends. The idea was to have coffee and some cake. It happened to be a religious festival. The café was closed. We unadvisedly decided to ride to our next point of interest, the Randa Monastery, 20 kilometres further on. About 15 kilometres later, we hit a stretch of road covered in debris from a hedge-cutting tractor. Do you occasionally do things against your better judgement? Since retiring, this seems to be a recurring theme for me, and it's becoming a habit I must get out of. As soon as I saw it my brain said stop, but my legs said go. Dom was just ahead, floating above this bed of thorns. He had been extolling the virtues of his beloved tubeless tyres only 10 minutes earlier; that should also have rung alarm bells. About 1 hour later, we had just finished fixing puncture number eleven. We did not have enough inner tubes between us, so new additions to our tour kit—Leznye Smart Puncture Repair Patches—were so easy to use and so effective. Thanks, Lisa, for saving the day!

Now, I'm hungry and dehydrated, time for another instance of 'against my better judgement'. This is the time to turn back; it's one of those days when things are not going right. The group had decided not to do the climb up to Randa Monastery but to ride to the village of Randa, 5 kilometres further on, where there's a café. I think if we're not doing the climb, we should turn back now, save 10 kilometres, and get refreshments back in the last town. I didn't shout loudly enough. We struggled to Randa. You know what's coming: the café is closed. Once we had recalibrated and settled our thoughts, we bade farewell to our friends, and we set off on our return journey, aiming first for a town about 10 kilometres away (but on the return journey) that we hoped would have a café. It did. We sat in the sweltering heat and enjoyed a pleasant, though very late, lunch.

We were relieved that we just had the cycle back to do and the worst was over, but it wasn't. The more direct route that we were taking turned out to have long sections of gravel roads that we had not expected. I was complaining about them (even though I had planned the route), but Dom was saying how much he liked them and that he was enjoying the ride. About 20 minutes later, Dom hit a rock as he went 'round a corner, bringing him down with a thump. Parts of his bike were pointing in the wrong direction (back the way we had come), his saddle was bent and twisted (a bit like Dom, actually), his tyre was torn and punctured, and he had blood flowing from cuts on his arms and thighs. All in all, he was not looking in a good way.

What Dom did, though, was not panic (even though he only had us a lot to help him.) He brushed himself down, then up, sorted his bike out with some help from us, and then steadily cycled back to his hotel (at least 30 kilometres) with us in support. We arrived back to find Sarah, his wife, in a deckchair, drinking gin and tonic. I was worried that Sarah may have been worrying about what had happened to him, "You probably got an automated alarm from Dom's Garmin warning that there had been an incident; are you okay?" "John, I knew you were all with him, and I was on my third gin and tonic, what is there to worry about?"

Two other alterations to our touring kit were made following chats with other cyclists on the Mallorca trip. One was to take some straps instead of cable ties for emergencies, and the second was to get some mountain bike shoes and pedals. One of the straps came into good use within the first 10 days when my trousers kept slipping down (what a dick) as a belt! The mountain bike shoes turned out to have been a very wise decision, with the regular need to walk across uneven ground.

The weekend before our departure, we also spent a few days cycling with the club. San Fairy Ann Cycling Club tour to Costa Blanca. There were about 40 members taking part in this following last year's successful Mont Ventoux trip. It was a bit close to the start of our tour 'round France, but we couldn't resist it. A useful warm-up? Well, it was fast and there was plenty of climbing with a great bunch of cyclists. It didn't seem to do us any harm!

Who is, or what is, San Fairy Ann?

The club's unusual name goes back to when it was founded in 1922.

The founder members had returned from serving in the forces during the 1914–1918 war.

They met at the Anchor Inn at Yalding and had difficulty deciding on an appropriate name.

Someone said, "San Fairy Ann," which was a soldier's phrase from the war and an anglicisation of the French 'Ca ne fait rien', meaning "It doesn't matter."

(As I write, Kate and I are privileged enough to be joint presidents.)

Not Testing Out Your Kit and Bike Before the Event

Oh, come on, it's a bit obvious, isn't it? Would you run a marathon in a new pair of running shoes? Or without putting Vaseline on your nipples? (I have considered some voluntary work in the last few miles of a marathon and stood with a tub of Vaseline in case there is anyone in need.) You really need to be as comfortable as possible on the bike; your kit needs to be comfortable; and your baggage needs to be fitted securely and safely (she's on the seat behind me.) The first day, riding with all your gear should not be the day you set off. There's a good chance that even then, you will experience some mechanical mishap. We planned a fully loaded ride (without the cheese) from home to Whitstable, about a 100-kilometre round trip, a few weeks before setting off. As we ascended a climb, our gear jammed, and then the chain came off. I also noticed that our rear light had failed. So, it became a 50-kilometre ride instead of 100. But now, including a trip to our local bike shop, Senacre Cycles, they got our gear running smoothly, and a new rear light was also purchased. A successful test ride.

Even if there isn't anything noticeably wrong with your bike, it is always worth getting it serviced before your ride to make sure there are no underlying problems and to make the bike as efficient as possible. Senacre Cycles did a thorough service on our tandem prior to this tour. I briefed them to check everything and replace anything showing signs of wear. I also advised on any spare parts we should take where things are unlikely to last up to 8,000 kilometres. We might as well have bought another tandem to tow behind us on a trailer! But then we'd have needed a spare trailer as well. We still made some changes to our setup on the journey due to not totally taking my own advice!

Wait to Eat/Drink Until You Feel Hungry/Thirsty at Your Peril

Food and drink are your fuel; you don't want to run out of energy, and it's important to fuel effectively. During multi-day events, you need to ride at an intensity you can sustain over the course of the event. That said, this is something that is so much easier said than done. People we cycle with cannot believe (and worry about) our low level of fluid intake, arriving at a lunch break having barely drunk a bidon (une bouteille d'eau) of fluid between us. In the right conditions, such as heat still weather up Mont Ventoux or Mount Teide, our fluid intake does, thankfully, dramatically change to compensate. You should never wait until you feel hungry, of course, or you risk running out of energy or 'bonking'. Eating and drinking little and often is the best strategy to ensure you replace the calories you are burning. Bonking is something that I have suffered from more than Kate, and it tends to follow a pattern. Which reluctantly brings me to my Passo dello Stelvio story.

This story starts with breakfast, if possible, even a second breakfast. In J.R.R. Tolkien's tales about Hobbits are specifically described as eating six meals a day when they can get them. They would probably have made excellent cyclists, albeit on balance bikes. It sort of starts without breakfast. I have a particular challenge when riding multiple days; after about the third day, I struggle to even look at breakfast, let alone eat it. I know I need to eat something, so I will try to come up with something different, more continental than full English, for example. Typically, it results in me not taking on enough fuel. I'm blaming the event in question on Polka Dot Cycling (an outstanding cycling touring company that is unfortunately no longer there), and it's always good to deflect the blame elsewhere. We had cycled a few hard days of climbing and then had a day when we were to cycle from Merano in the South Tyrol region of Italy to Bormio in the province of Sondrio. This would involve cycling one of the most iconic passes in cycling, the Stelvio. Although we would have to cycle about 50 kilometres to the base of the climb, we were advised it's a fairly flat ride with just one gentle incline.

At this point, I should introduce you to Stu from 'Polka Dot Cycling', whose favourite phrase would be, the hotel is next right, "just up a cheeky little climb," which could, in fact, be a couple of kilometres long with a 20% gradient.

I should have had this in mind that morning, but no. You live and learn, okay, perhaps not learn. We hit the first gentle incline after, well, after nothing. Fair enough, gentle it was, only 2 or 3 percent for a few kilometres. That would be it, though, wouldn't it be the perfect example of an actual gentle incline? Nope, this was obviously one of those false flats. This false flat led us into another 3-kilometre climb, averaging 5%. It's not steep by any means, but if you ignore the 10% section, I recall switchbacks being thrown in for good measure. I felt strangely lethargic being so early into a ride, but hey ho! I seem to recall Stu saying something along the lines of, "I don't remember that having such a kick," (bloody liar), "but we are now on a plateau for the next 15 kilometres, so let's push on." I recall glancing around me and thinking how stunning the area was, but struggling to really enjoy it as I couldn't get into a rhythm, and what a shame that this flat plateau was uphill all the way!

One good thing about starting to bonk is that you can do something about it just eat. Luckily, after this long drag, we arrived in a village with a patisserie, and Jen had been shopping (Jen is the brains and talent of the Polka Dot Cycling partnership.) She arrived with two massive trays of apple pie. I had two doorstops.

One bad thing about bonking is not knowing that you are. I didn't. The delicious pie I had eaten was, of course, temporarily helpful, but retrospectively, it was replacing a deficit of fuel rather than providing the energy to tackle a significant climb. We still had to get there. The next hour or two of cycling was a continuous drag-up hill, probably never more than 3%, but still a continuous drain on the resources. By the time we had reached the town at the start of the climb, a feeling of lethargy was beginning to creep in. It's probably a sign that things aren't right! Now it might be helpful; I know what you're thinking (or perhaps you've forgotten that Kate is sitting behind me?) to communicate with Kate and let her know that things don't feel good—or at least don't feel quite right. Nope, at this point I may not be feeling that I 'have the legs' today, but that bonking issue is cleverly sneaking up on me without me realising it. What is this Passo dello Stelvio, climb then? If you are a cyclist, you don't need to tell anyone. If not, then you may have heard of Mont Ventoux or the Alpe d'Huez (or maybe Box Hill?)—the Stelvio is a similarly revered climb.

Distance: 24.5 kilometres; Elevation gain: 1824 metres; that is a lot in one go.

The climb is categorised as Hors Categorie* with an average of 7.5% and 10% max and a massive altitude of 2758m (oxygen deficit territory.)

The first few kilometres go well; we are riding steadily, not pushing it because there's a long way to go. But it's not long before I begin to feel slow; feeling lethargically lethargic is the best way to call it. Even Dom overtakes us! We plod on, and our speed drops from up to 15kph to below 10kph. I'm a little disappointed; the climb should be something to take in and remember, but after 10 kilometres, I'm beginning to struggle to turn my legs around.

I'm beginning to feel Kate's power pushing the pedals. The road has been steadily making its way upwards with very little deviation. Perhaps one or two hairpins, but mainly straight. At this point, whilst not actually feeling very hungry, I ask Kate if we have anything, and she passes forward a handful of peanuts. Shortly after we reached the first set of switchbacks, in some woods, if I recall. At this point, the Polka Dot Cycling minibus is waiting to offer fluids, advice, sweets, clothing, baguettes, and crisps; they almost force feed you, "Do you need anything? Food? Drink." I'm not sure what happens here; only Mr Bonk can explain, but even my voice is lethargic. I just heard Kate reply, "No, we are fine; just had some peanuts."

Well, that was it, wasn't it, or perhaps that wasn't it? The opportunity to retrieve the situation had gone. Not that I truly understood that there was a situation that needed retrieving, and Kate obviously had not yet noticed that her autopilot was beginning to malfunction. My memory of much of the rest of the climb is a bit vague.

I recall two sets of switchbacks (I was not feeling great, but I wanted to remember them.)

I remember Kate asking me if everything was okay (she had noticed that I was not taking my share of power output on each pedal stroke, no doubt.)

I remember some stunning snow-covered views (I said to myself, "I must remember those stunning snow-covered views.")

I remember crying more than once (I would call it sobbing disguised as sniggering.)

---

* *Hors catégorie (HC) is a climb that is 'beyond categorisation'. The term was originally used for those mountain roads where cars could not get up. The HC climb is the most difficult type of climb in a race such as the Tour de France.*

I remember each switch back presenting another stretch of road, and that road moving very slowly beneath the tandem and saying, "What's the matter with this road?"

A couple of kilometres from the summit, Jen (the clever one) cycled down to meet us and ride a few bends with us. I now realise they were probably concerned about us; they knew us well enough and probably thought we were rather sluggish (snail-ish). She was holding a conversation with Kate which pleased me as I was hoping she hadn't noticed that I was sobbing (ha!). She then went back on up ahead of us. I remember being very sad about that, but I didn't know why. As we reached the summit, Stu appeared, jogging beside us and started giving me instructions. I was half expecting him to say, 'just 'round the corner and up a cheeky little climb', but instead he said, "John, don't stop. There's a car park on the left, turn into it and do a circuit. Do you understand?" I nodded. "You may not be able to uncleat, as you come around, ride to a stop between us and we'll catch you."

I did as I was instructed, cycled in between two rows of cyclists and then just felt them grab hold of us. What had happened—had someone superglued my cleats onto the pedals and owned up to Stu before we reached the top? (Dom?)

I remember Kate laughing. That's not true; I recall someone commenting about Kate laughing. If it was true, I understood that. Sobbing wasn't something I did; emotions have unexpected effects on our reactions. Someone was very concerned for my health (not me, Dom, I think; he was probably being sarcastic).

Stu explained that this was what real bonking looked like, and he was also passing me things to eat whilst keeping me standing over the tandem. Then, when Stu deemed me ready, a couple of cyclists helped me off the tandem and into the minibus as they deemed me unfit to go down the other side of the mountain, evidently even unfit enough to get myself to and in the minibus! (Kate at this time was going from one person to another looking for a volunteer pilot to take her down the mountain…she wasn't successful!)

The good thing about all of this is the opportunity to learn from it and attempt not to make the same mistake again, starting with a good breakfast!

Breakfast doesn't need to be discussed, but if you are British, there's one thing we need to agree on (if you are a Hobbit, you are exempt from this.)

Dinner, though, is the main meal of the day. It's a moveable feast and may be taken during the day or the evening. It's very simple. It's a fact. Like the fact that the earth is a globe.

Lunch and tea are words used for the top-up meal. So, lunch—for when dinner is going to be taken later in the day. Tea is for when dinner has already been consumed earlier in the day. Consequently, either lunch or tea may not exist on any given day! Supper, snack, and brunch are bonus foods. Sorted. I have a feeling there could be some days on this trip when we get breakfast and tea, but little lunch and no dinner!

Not Checking the Weather Forecast

It's important that you check the weather and know the terrain you will be riding on so that you can pack the appropriate kit. (So my rule about avoiding gravel roads makes part of the decision for us.) Ideally, you will pack for all weather eventualities because the cycling kit is designed to be squeezed into small bags to allow for multi-day riding where the weather will vary. The worst thing you can do is be too hot or too cold whilst out on your bike. Prevent this by packing wind jackets, arm and leg warmers, and waterproofing if there's a chance of rain. Your temperature on the bike can change quickly; for example, you may get hot and sweaty climbing a mountain, but at the top it's likely to be much cooler. On the descent, the wind chill picks up, and it can indeed become very chilly! For me, the best approach is to have clothes that can be worn under or over other clothes. Wearing layers is the best way to stay warm, but it also provides flexibility to wear fewer clothes when needed. By the way, the temperature is measured in Celsius in the book because I am English.

The Bike

Oops, I nearly forgot, "Don't forget, some people like to know about the bike, John." You will have picked up that it's a tandem—one of the best options if one of you is visually impaired, though only assuming they ride on the back. We often get asked by people if we take turns deciding who goes on the front/back. I just give one of my silent, blank stares and leave Kate to answer. We have a choice of 4 tandems, but we could do with another (N+1, N being the number of tandems you own, +1 being the number you 'need').

(For pictures, go to Facebook: Snails around France.)

1. A Butler time trial tandem. Suitable only for time trialling with a disc wheel on the back, aerodynamic armrests on the front, and gears that will only manage a 3% incline (possibly 20% if it's only 1 metre long, you get a run up, and the finish line is at the crest of the climb, allowing you to crumble into a heap of uselessness.) It's also a short wheelbase, meaning that Kate can't stand, or her knees will hit my buttocks (if they could navigate her handlebars), and her nose is shoved up my arse. You can just smell the fear (well, she can.)
2. A Cannondale 29er mountain bike tandem. Nice big wheels with big tyres that would get down forest tracks. It has a wide range of gears and looks great but weighs a lot. It would be great at carrying gear; possibly towing a trailer or caravan would definitely get us there, but probably quite a few days longer. Our cycling has often been focused on speed and aerodynamics, and we haven't psychologically moved to this type of touring yet, but it would have got us closer to some of the borders and provided new experiences. One day, we'll get on it and ride into the sunset, stopping just before it gets too dark.
3. A carbon fibre 'Landescape' in our club colours. The frame is made by Cyfac (a renowned frame builder based in Hommes, France), and it has Enve carbon wheels. It is so beautiful that it hangs on our dining room wall! No, I can't bring myself to load that up with touring gear, but it's great for fine-weather riding, supported trips, club rides, and sportives.

4. Not so different in style is our aluminium Landescape with a carbon belt drive (which was originally on tandem 3). We have used it on most of our tours. It travels well, has a great range of gears, places to fit pannier racks, and still looks very good. Easy choice, really.

Applying for a Visa

I'm sad to have to include this section, which has become necessary due to Brexit. But I will just reflect on our visa experience, something we would not have needed if people in the UK had voted to remain in the European Union. I really think they could have checked with me; I'm no scaremonger!

We have gone through our lives regularly visiting France and enjoying the freedom of movement that being a part of Europe allows. We now find that if we want to spend a few months cycling around France, then we need a visa.

The extra cost is one thing—the application for us was altogether a bit of a challenge. This section is purely from my own experience. If you are used to applying for visas, then the process is possibly more straightforward, and there may be short cuts, and some of this would now be obvious. This is how it went for me as a virgin—touched for the very first time. What I thought I knew.

- We would be in France for less than 90 days, which meant that we would not need a long-stay visa.
- I could apply for a visa 6 months before needed.
- It was likely to cost around £50.

I wanted this all sorted (stress-free), so I worked on the visa in November, 7 months ahead of our trip. I had to go to a French Visa website to complete the application. First, register an account to use the site, and then collect the information needed.

I discovered that I had to complete two applications, one for each of us. You'd think, just one tandem, a married couple…oh, never mind.

I then discovered that I would need a long-stay visa. The visa isn't for 90+ consecutive days, but 90+ days within a rolling 180-day period. Damn, we shouldn't have booked that 10-day trip to Mallorca in spring and that 4-day cycling club trip to Costa Blanca the week before our tour starts! (Yeah, okay, so it might be obvious to you.)

Anyway, applications are complete, and I now just need to wait until the 6 months to go alarm goes off and submit my application.

6 months to go came at last. I logged on and submitted my application, and I was then directed to another service to register another account and input 2 new sets of information about each of us and our reference numbers for our original applications. It's all done, and I go to press submit when I discover:

1. Only short-term visas can be applied for 6 months in advance.
2. Long-term visas need to be applied for no more than 3 months in advance.
   Logically, that makes no sense to me, but okay, now we need to wait another 3 months.
3. Months passed and, of course, the website had not retained my information, so I had to do it all again with multiple attempts for it to accept and then remember a password. Nonetheless, I finally hit the submit button, which took me to a calendar of times and dates to book an appointment in London.
4. I was expecting this.
5. I wasn't expecting it to be booked up for 4 weeks to 10 days before our Mallorca trip. (I have a feeling that some block booking may have taken place by commercial organisations, but absolutely no proof of that!)

This created a problem. I was advised that the process takes about 15 working days, especially for long-term visas. I won't get our passports back in time for the Mallorca trip.

I therefore chose to book an appointment for the first day back after our Mallorca trip. It was a very stressful situation that I did not want to be in. This would now give time for the return of our passports and visas, with 22 days until our Spanish trip and 28 days until our tour begins. Needlessly stressful. Or am I needlessly stressed? Either way, the word stress is in there somewhere!

Having gone through this process, I think I would now hit the submit button in advance of the 3-month date, as I wouldn't be surprised if the official submission date is not actually until the appointment takes place. I could then have gotten an earlier appointment. I don't know if that would work. (If you are keeping up with this, then you could actually survive the rest of this book!)

The cost? About a £33 fee each, presumably to the company for the appointment, and 99 euros each for the visa. I didn't vote for Brexit, but I sure am, literally, paying the price (which would eventually prove to be more expensive; do read on.)

Please grab a drink and take a seat. The interview date arrived, and we were due to attend an interview at 2 p.m. (Just a reminder that this was our first visa experience, and we don't know if it's normal. So, it only reflects our experience.)

We arrived at 1.30 and joined a queue to have key papers checked at the front desk (Passport: Tick; Application form: Tick.) Phew, good start. (Don't assume your visit will be fun. We immediately notice a rather unpleasant attitude by many staff whose communication is a mixture of condescending, short-tempered, and impatient with anyone whose responses are not immediately as they require or who ask what they seem to deem as 'silly' questions.) A number of fellow applicants were visibly dismayed and stressed by the atmosphere.

Approximately, at 2 p.m. we joined a waiting room to be called to our appointment at a counter. Then, at 2.15, we are called to the counter. I wear a hearing aid and have trouble hearing the questions that the agent asks through a perspex shield, so as she becomes impatient with my responses, I explain this (ironically, I'm not sure if she hears me—or doesn't acknowledge it.) Kate is standing next to me with her guide dog, struggling to read and write information passed to her (Kate, not the guide dog.) "What do you want a long-term visa for?"

"We are cycling 'round the whole of France, about 7,500 kilometres."

She looks at our passport-style photos and says, "You've got glasses on!" She tells us that our photos are no good because we have glasses on. At the end of (the online application process, provided detailed information about the photo and we both recall that glasses are fine as long as there are no reflections. I have glasses on my passport. We spent a good deal of time composing and recomposing the photo until it appeared close to the examples.) But we are both over eighty, so perhaps our memories are confused.

We were then asked for printouts of where we were staying (I had only provided info for the first night). We will be staying in over 80 different hotels! "Why are you staying in so many hotels?" Honestly, I promise, I did not do the blank stare at the camera. "Because we are cycling right 'round France and need somewhere to stay each night…" The advisor insists that we need to print out confirmation emails for every night, twice (a copy for each of our applications.)

"...you can either go home and then arrange a new appointment with your documents or pay £10 to be provided with a place to do it here." We chose to do it here.

"Now go through the door on the left for biometrics." At about 2.45 p.m., we enter a waiting room for biometrics. No explanation of what to expect. About 70 people waiting, and we decided, without direction or support, to sit amongst them. It feels like something out of a dystopian 'big brother' style movie. As we sit there, observing and working out the process, it becomes evident that groups of applicants are called by appointment time (they are only just calling 1 p.m. appointments, and at least 10 applicants scramble to join and form a queue, so this could be a long wait; the whole thing seems so primitive.)

We get called at about 3.30, and at this point, a person decides we go to the front of this queue due to the guide dog (I considered saying 'no need' but the words failed to come out.)

Biometrics complete (fingerprints, eye scans, and anal diameter measured), and now we go to retake our photos (£8 each) and return them to the biometrics lady, who is now holding a red-hot poker.

It's now about 4 p.m. and the place closes at 4.30, so we quickly go to an allocated computer (with a printer shared with two other computers) to print out our documents. We are printing out pages and pages of confirmation emails from our pre-booked accommodation. Amongst our printouts we are finding other individuals' bank statements, travel arrangements, and inside leg measurements as they print to the same machine. We have asked several staff members whether what we are doing makes any sense (and can you load more printer paper again, please), and all responses indicate that, whilst they have never seen it before, if that is what has been asked for, then that is what is needed. Literally no staff we asked had seen anyone doing this, and yet everyone said you need to do as you have been asked. I can see problems with this.

We complete this task at about 7 p.m. Did you say 7 p.m.? I did. I know that I said it closes at 4.30 p.m., but it also seems that once you have started, they let you finish! We are the only customers remaining and have been for about an hour. Kate's guide dog sat at our feet the whole time. (Is she still alive? The guide dog, not Kate, though obviously that as well.) We hand in the completed documents to the remaining advisor on duty.

"What have you got there?" the agent's jaw dropped upon seeing the pile of papers, and once we have explained what we have been asked to do, he has to ask his boss how to process it as he has never seen such a pack of documents. The supervisor also seems somewhat perplexed that we have been asked to do this. They have never come across so much printing; "the £10 won't even have covered the cost." (good, though a bit irrelevant as everyone needing extra evidence pays £10 and most seem to only need a page or two.) Unsure how to progress, they say they'll need to consult with the consulate and will call us tomorrow. We get home at 10.30 p.m. stopping for an incredibly rare McDonald's on the way home. I'm worried.

The following day, no return call came. I called them late afternoon, but an advisor could find no issue on our account (in fact, he suggests that their comment about calling the consulate makes no sense as it is this organisation that decides what goes in a pack!) He advised that he had sent an email to chase the return call. At about 6.30 p.m., I received two emails requesting we return to the centre. 1. Because biometric information is needed (we did that yesterday as described); 2. Because the date is wrong (no explanation of which date.) Also, there is no explanation as to whether we can just turn up or whether we must book an appointment. Our first booking was 4 weeks later than I wanted because the slots were fully booked up, so I am now becoming worried that if this goes wrong, we'll run out of time.

First thing in the morning, day three, I call the centre to check if I must make an appointment to follow up on my emails. Thankfully, as I have been 'invited' (sounds like the police inviting you to visit your local police station), I can just turn up. Unfortunately, for our 2-year-old grandson, Rudy, it means he also gets to visit—at least the guide dog gets a break this time!

We are taken straight to the counter, where an agent checks our case and advises that Kate's name is wrong. (I have always had doubts about her. Exactly who is this person that hops onto the back of my bike and fakes contributing to the wattage required to get us over the next mountain?)

"I always thought you were called Kathy; when did it change to Kate?"

"John, don't be silly."

So, what's the issue? The agent explained that our application included Kate's middle name, but her passport didn't (a surprise, as neither of us had noticed when it was renewed a few years ago.)

"Can we change it?"

"Yes, you can, but you need to go home and reapply!"

"What? But that won't give us enough time to get our visa in time."

"I'm sorry, I can't help that."

"So, you've invited us to travel 2 hours to get here just to be told this? This couldn't have been an email or a phone call."

After further discussion (Kate called it "cross, but not aggressive"), I let go of his throat, and the agent sought advice from his supervisor and gained permission to work with us to complete the application. The agent is very diligent and, gradually, friendly. After about 2 hours, the job is complete, and two very bulky applications are slammed onto the floor by the agent in a sense of triumph, "Done!"

Though he does a double take and notices my passport has crawled out, and is sat laughing at him on his desk. Rubber bands are quickly removed and the passport puts up a fight but is forced back inside and sorted.

What a relief it was to get back home. However, it was going to be a long wait—about 15 working days for the decision. At last, though, something went smoothly; having paid a further £18 for our passports to be sent to us, they arrived just 1 week later…and our passports contained our visas. Phew!

The Stoker

Okay then, a bit about the stoker. If you plan to cycle 'round France on a tandem, they are an equal part of the adventure!

I was clearing some books for a charity shop and came across Kate's book, 'Recycling Me'. It made me realise I hadn't said much about her part in our tour 'round France.

If you don't ride a tandem, you may not know what a stoker is. It's simple; it's the rider at the back of the tandem. The rider at the front is the pilot (or captain.) Riding at the rear, the stoker is an essential contributor to the tandem's motion rather than a passenger with their feet up at the back. Humans are actually fairly predictable beings, and the thousands that call out, "She's not pedalling," or the like, are in fact far from the truth. We have to put on a fake laugh to make them feel they are original.

Ideally, the stoker needs strength and endurance and an awareness of when extra power is quickly needed to help get over a hill and be able to provide that power. The stoker needs to know how to lean into a turn and to move smoothly on the back so as not to unbalance the tandem. Other roles can be negotiated (such as signalling, passing food forward, telling the pilot what to do, etc.)

We ride a tandem because Kate had a serious accident whilst cycling back in 2013, which resulted in a traumatic brain injury. Not a fun time. It was unclear for the first couple of weeks whether she would survive. It occurred to me that we would both want to continue cycling, so when I knew she would be coming home 4 or 5 months later, I bought a tandem, balanced her on the back, and off we went! She had no choice; at the time, I had to do most things for her, so she just did what I said. (One consequence of the accident was that she only knew she had a cycling accident because we told her, you know those films when someone is living a lie following an accident and those around her know that it wasn't really a bike accident? It wasn't one of them.) By the way, she was convinced she was 21 years old. Sadly, she also seemed to think we had 3 children, and even more sadly, we have 4. Her book was as much about her going through the process of putting her thoughts on paper about the accident and tells that story at quite a personal level.

I won't describe all of the effects the accident had on Kate, but the most challenging were: visual impairments (she now has a white stick and a guide dog, but luckily some useful vision); difficulties with memory and balance; difficulty coming to terms with the impact of the accident (also difficulty with memory and balance.)

But Kate also had, and still has perseverance, stamina, power, and competitiveness.

The greatest benefit of cycling to Kate is probably the same for all of us: our mental health. The tandem has enabled her to continue with her love of cycling, and me, of course.

Kate only has a few specific needs for the tour.

1. The tandem!
2. A place to carry and quickly access her white stick (a telescopic stick and extra bike pump holder work perfectly.)
3. Me—for whatever else comes up.
4. Me—for whatever else doesn't come up.
5. Someone to provide her guide dog with a nice holiday (Sarah, one of our daughters—the forgotten child!).

Otherwise, we are just a couple who love cycling (and each other, of course.) By the way, cycling 'round France was her idea.

The Journey
Ready? Go!

(I know, at last!) My story of the tour is divided into cycling days.

Each day identifies the distance and elevation that was covered that day (well, as measured by my Garmin), and running totals for these are in brackets, along with the place of departure, the destination, the weather (temp is in Celsius), and food eaten by me (it's my book). Then a description of some places visited or passed and events that took place.

Getting to France: 26th May 2023, distance: 81.78 kilometres (10 kilometres of which in France), elevation gain: 874 metres.

Depart: Maidstone, England Arrive: Graveline, France Weather: Sunny 22 degrees, but with a cold headwind.

Food: Porridge, fruit bagels, banana, tuna sandwich, double chicken burger, frite, side salad. (Weight John: 70.6 kg, Kate: 57.0 kg—just so when we get back, we can answer questions like, 'Did you lose weight from all that cycling?' like we didn't eat.)

I wondered if we would get to the ferry in time. 1 p.m. last check-in sounds too early. This trip was not supposed to be stressful. I'm retired; this should be relaxed and enjoyable. But you can't miss your ferry can you? It should only take about 3½ hours to get to Dover (70 kilometres), so leave by 9.30 a.m. What if we have a puncture? Okay, leave by 9 a.m. Phew, that suddenly seems so much better. We left at 8 a.m.; I explained to David that it makes sense to move straight to French time (yes, I know).

Tandem is suitably loaded, David's bike, surprisingly not unsuitably overloaded, and we cruise along excited and relaxed. A steady climb or two on the A20 after Charing leaves us more breathless than they should have, and then a couple of hours later, the steeper climb up onto the Downs near Folkestone (Dover Hill) begins to question our ability for the adventure ahead. Slow, a bit of a drag, a little too sweaty, a little breathless, and a little early in the tour. Kate stood up and pushed hard most of the way up!

I wondered when we'd have dinner today. Perhaps on the ferry, or that could be lunch. Perhaps in Gravelines, or that could be tea. Just saying.

Our cycling buddy, David Butterworth, had joined us and would be cycling with us for most of the first week to Cherbourg. Neither of us recall who invited him, so we just agreed to blame each other. David is part Hobbit; if allowed, he stops to eat whenever the possibility arises. (He's not quite as cute as a Hobbit, though.) Our cycle from home needed a day to include the ferry. Quite a luxury to be able to set off loaded up and not wonder if you have forgotten something or taken too much! Though we realised that we'd never left our house for so long before.

I know that the older generation (probably my own perception, I accept) turns off water, electricity, and gas; puts up razor wire on their gates; places trip wires on their pathway; and leaves a key under the mat for the neighbours to check the house if the alarm goes off (which it does when the neighbours nip in for a sip of the sherry stocks and realise they haven't been provided with the alarm deactivation protocol.) So, to play safe, we left a key under the mat with no warning that instead of an alarm, anyone entering gets arrows shot out from the walls, plus a giant iron ball thunders down the hallway towards them.

Kent is a great place to cycle if you watch out for potholes, varied terrain, beautiful countryside, and operation Brexit Gridlock (Brock), just some of the local attractions, and we had them all today. The route took us east from Maidstone towards Folkestone and onwards to Dover. Catching the ferry and staying near Dunkerque for that night would mean we got the hassle out of the way and could get on with our first day's ride first thing in the morning.

When you cycle off the ferry, it's either fun or daunting. I couldn't decide. But you are amongst traffic trying to get on with their journeys, eager to join motorways, and at first you wonder if you might be sucked onto a motorway with them. But you can very quickly move onto fast, flat roads and cycle tracks if you know where they are. Our route was up the road; turn right at the first opportunity and head for Calais. To follow the route meant starting the official day one route of SaF (Snails around France), which was rewarding as it meant that day 1 (tomorrow) was going to be about 10 kilometres shorter. Ahead of schedule already, we might manage to do this thing!

Gravelines was a surprise to me. A strange, non-French-looking name (though less so if pronounced properly, Grav-leen, I'm guessing.) I had in mind an industrial suburb of Calais. In fact, there's a lot more to it (let alone being about 20 kilometres from Calais), with impressive buildings such as the rather grand tower (Belfry) in the centre, the town square, the arsenal, sea defences, and a canal linking Saint Omer to the sea. The peacefully walled town of Gravelines is surprisingly unspoilt by the wars and still retains a great deal of French architecture. In the city itself, I believe there are also boat rides on the canals to enjoy.

"Do you know anything about this place, David?"

"Actually, a few things. There was a meeting here in 1520, if I recall, between the Holy Roman Emperor Charles V and Henry VIII of England. There were a few battles fought nearby, including a naval attack using fire ships in about 1588, launched by the Royal Navy against the Spanish Armada at anchor."

"Really?"

"There's more—before that, in the early 12th century, Saint Omer was an important port in western Flanders, but silting gradually cut it off from the North Sea, so they built a canal to the new coast at what is now Gravelines. The name is derived from the Dutch Gravenenga, meaning Count's Canal. The new town became heavily fortified as it guarded the western borders of Spanish territory in Flanders." This is what David contributes to our cycling holidays: unbelievable knowledge with an emphasis on unbelievable.

(What David actually said was, "Err, no, nothing.")

Ooh, I must mention that we spotted our first 'chateau d'eau' today. You know, those things we call water towers in England? They are called Castles of Water in France, which I love. I had to stop beside it for a 'fontaine de pipi'.

<u>Day 1</u>, 27th May, distance: 131.30 kilometres (141.30 kilometres), elevation gain: 874m (905m) Depart: Graveline. Arrive: Fort-Mahon-Plage.

Weather: Sunny 22 degrees with a helpful tail wind.

Food: Croissants, yoghurt, fruit, baguette, granary bread, sardines, a tuna sandwich (eaten in a supermarket car park with stunt planes flying overhead), bananas, prawns, frites, and steak with shallots—that's shallot.

What is perhaps surprising is that the ferry to Dunkerque avoids Dunkerque! Dunkerque Ferry Port is located at Loon-Plage, west of Dunkerque. So, we won't enter Dunkerque until the end of our journey. Having stayed the night at Gravelines, we are now on schedule. ("On schedule? How dare you use that phrase!"—an anonymous angry world traveller.)

So, the first significant place we have passed is in fact Calais (sorry, Graveline, I did try to raise awareness of your merits, but David let you down with his amazing ability to contribute so little.) Calais overlooks the Strait of Dover, the narrowest point in the English Channel, which is only 34 kilometres wide here, and is the closest French town to England. The White Cliffs of Dover can easily be seen on a clear day from Calais (strangely, the same cannot be said if you are on the other side looking back across, mainly because they would be under your feet.) Calais is a major port for ferries between France and England, and since 1994, the Channel Tunnel (yes, a tunnel!) has linked nearby Coquelles to Folkestone by rail. They have trains that you drive on and off (no, you can't cycle through; wouldn't that be great…don't be silly; it wouldn't, would it?) The north coast of France appears to be characterised by wide sandy beaches and sand dunes. It is beautiful to look at, but it can be a bit windy, as far as I can tell. Theoretically, tandems are good—well better than solo bikes—if it's a headwind, because the stoker (Kate) is shielded from the headwind—assuming she's got her head down. "Have you got your head down?"

"No."

"Why not?"

"Because you asked me a question."

Beyond Calais, just like the coast of England, which can be seen just across the water, the sandy beaches are replaced with chalky cliffs and small harbours; you'd think that England had snapped off from mainland Europe. A good walking area, I imagine, it is also like the southeastern coast of England. We soon return to a flat area with sandy beaches and Le Touquet, which is known for its sand dunes.

I was a bit grateful that, having started at Graveline, we had 10 kilometres less to do today and a tail wind. We rode well, arriving about 2 hours earlier than we had feared!

Just before Etaples, we spotted a military cemetery that contained 10,771 Commonwealth burials from the First World War, the earliest dating from May 1915. 35 of these burials were unidentified young men. We can do the things we do thanks to the sacrifice of these people.

Fort Mahon-Plage mainly consisted of one high street, which led directly to the beach. The high street had shops, bars, and restaurants on each side, and we were able to find a nice restaurant to replace the calories we had burned off today! When we arrived at the restaurant, we were advised that food wasn't available until 6.30 (it was 5.30). Kate and I had a Belgian beer to relax with until the restaurant was open, but David, having worked his socks off to secure us a table, decided that a banana split was the order of the day, thus further demonstrating his Hobbit-like tendencies, including not wearing socks.

<u>Day 2</u>, 28th May, distance: 138.10 kilometres (279.40 kilometres), elevation gain: 940m (1,845m).

Depart: Fort-Mahon-Plage. Arrive: Veulettes-Sur-Mer.

Weather: Sunny 22 degrees with the same tailwind or a close relative.

Food: Croissants; bread rolls; fruit cocktails; peanuts; baguette sandwiches (ham/cheese); antipasto vegetables; margarita pizza.

After the first flat 40 kilometres, we climbed into the hills of the Somme, and whilst on top, we had fast, long, and flat roads but then frequently plummeted down into pleasant coastal bays before having to find steep climbs back out again. Kate prefers going uphill, so she was happy, whilst David was pleased that apart from the uphill, it was all downhill. Before we climbed into the hills, we cycled through Saint-Valery-Sur-Somme. Initially taking a wrong turn just before a shared railway/road bridge, we travelled a short distance down a gravel track, ending up opposite the town but gaining a delightful view of it. The Baie de la Somme is a wetland habitat for birdlife, and there were groups of walkers down here with cameras and binoculars.

So, to get back to our route, we picked up speed and yelled out, "The English are coming," as we scattered them across the gravel road. The town is named after a monk who lived as a hermit on the headland from 611. It has a lot of history, including being the gathering place for William the Conqueror's fleet in 1066 and later the site of Joan of Arc's imprisonment by the English (hence my 'The English are coming' comment.)

It's a beautiful area, and it looked to be an interesting and inviting holiday destination. A mediaeval town, very pretty, but very busy with cars struggling around the one-way system.

Today we also passed Dieppe, a port at the mouth of the river Arques. We have passed through here a couple of times before, in particular when we cycled from home to Disneyland Paris with our family via Newhaven (the longest stage being from home to Newhaven.)

"Mum, can we go to Disneyland Paris?"

"Yes…if we cycle there!"

Dieppe is famous for its scallops. (Just to change the subject.)

"So, David, tomorrow it's the Pont de Normandie."

"Excellent, I love bridges."

"Not when you've cycled over this, you won't!" I said…perhaps to myself, though slightly impressed that he knew what a 'Pont' was. I checked with him though, "What's the Pont, David?"

"Oh, partly for fun but also to get away from the wife."

Today also felt a bit longish and rather sluggish, with an achey bottom and tight leg muscles. (Or was it achey leg muscles and a tight bottom?) Bit of a stiff neck as well. If I was aching, perhaps I had overestimated the fitness of my companions?

"How's it going, then?"

"Comfy, we seem to be zooming along," was the answer, almost in unison.

"Yes, that was what I was thinking—a brilliant start."

Veulettes-Sur-Mer wasn't the best of the bays we cycled down to. A slightly rundown resort but nonetheless with some nice restaurants, crashing Atlantic waves, and a pebble beach with impressive white, chalk cliffs at both ends of the beach.

We had a great evening meal, and after our main course, were asked if we wanted dessert.

David's reply was, "Jai, 'ave a look at the menu."

I tried not to laugh, but I failed miserably. The good thing, though, is that he makes the effort whilst we play safe.

Not sure exactly where, but we saw some other sights today. A clay pigeon shoot next to the road; a kite event with about 30 or more kites flying; sand-yachting on a beach; kite surfing in the sea; and David's bottom, as his lycra is wearing thin! I wonder which will be the most memorable, "Yeah, but the pad is really good" (some unwelcome images are difficult to unsee.)

Day 3, 29th May, distance 118.08 kilometres (397.48 kilometres), elevation gain 1,239m (2,084m).

Depart: Veulettes-Sur-Mer. Arrive: Honfleur.

Weather: Sunny 21 degrees, with an even stronger tailwind (big sister).

Food: c\Croissants, fruit, bread and jam, peanuts, tuna baguette, fish soup, duck leg, side salad, and frites; tarte au pomme.

Diving down into lovely bays, then back up through farmland, we passed through Le Havre today, which is situated at the mouth of the river Seine (scary bridge time.) Le Havre was rebuilt after World War II and you probably either love it or hate it with the concrete architecture designed by Auguste Perret, (the city centre is a UNESCO World Heritage Site, so you should at least respect it,

I guess!). Le Havre also has a beach and a picturesque marina, making it a surprisingly pleasant place to visit. The cycle lanes through the centre got us through easily and safely. We caught occasional glimpses of the bridge 'over there' but I had explained to Kate and David that we had to travel a good few kilometres away from Le Havre to follow a safe route back to the bridge (so if you know differently, please keep quiet.)

Towards the end of a long ride, that section was on a flat, straight road (at least 15 kilometres) into a headwind, and it began to drag. Kate was fortunate to be with me. I could keep reminding her that we were on the route, that the bridge was 'over there' and that we would eventually come back around to it on a quiet roadway. David, however, could not cope mentally with heading away from the bridge; he began to slow down and started to mutter to himself about his 'preciousss' or something. (Presumably, his everlasting chamois protruding through his sheer see-through chiffon hot pants) Eventually, when we were on our return journey to the bridge and it came into sight, he was so excited and somewhat deluded!

"I'm amazed; how did we get over the river? We didn't cross the bridge, did we?"

We hadn't; of course, there were a few kilometres back now to cross it.

"But it's over there; we're on the other side!" I calmly and somewhat condescendingly explained to David that the bridge was over there, but it hadn't moved, and we still needed to cross it.

"So why are we here?" My response, because we haven't gotten over there yet, probably didn't help to calm things down. I reminded him that I had explained about the route, that it was a long way to the bridge, that our destination was in Honfleur, just on the other side, and that we had not deviated from our route, so we had done no more than planned, but I knew that he was still not equating what I had said with what he thought he could see. The truth is, I was convincing myself at the same time; it did seem strange.

As we approach Normandy beaches, it's worth recalling that the city was bombarded during the Battle of Normandy, when 5,000 people were killed and 12,000 homes were destroyed before its capture. I seem to recall that the opportunity to evacuate civilians was declined by the allied forces, hopefully for the greater good.

Strange phrase that, "For the greater good." The history books explain that it is a translation of 'Für das Grö ßere Wohl' and was a phrase that Grindelwald used to justify the atrocities in the 1940s global wizarding war, and it was engraved over the Nurmengard prison entrance, which was constructed to house those who opposed him. It expressed his argument that what he was doing was eventually be to the benefit of everyone, apart from a small number of people that would suffer to bring about these benefits. So now you know.

That bridge. It's one of a number that, for the greater good, we need to cross. One of a number that triggers a certain degree of apprehension. Typically, bridges, and for that matter, tunnels that allow cyclists to pass, rarely consider safety, or even the impression of safety, to any reassuring degree.

The Pont de Normandie spans the river Seine, linking Le Havre to Honfleur. It's at least 2 kilometres long (or wide) and one of those amazing bridges to look at from the seat of a car that is, however, somewhat scarier from a cycling perspective. Although it is a toll bridge, it has a footpath/cycle lane in each direction, allowing pedestrians and cyclists to cross the bridge free of charge. After all, it would seem somewhat mean-minded to insist on a toll being paid just prior to your demise, or is that what's meant by a death toll? Anyway, as you approach the bridge head-on, it looks steep and threatening. There is a cycle lane, but it's not very wide, and there is no barrier between you and the possibility of becoming today's roadkill. But we got over it relatively easily with a great sense of relief! (David made some comments about not letting his wife know he'd gone over it. I was grateful we didn't have to let her know that he hadn't gotten over it.)

We were just downstream from Rouen. A famous place in cycling history as it was the finish of the first 'long distance' cycling race from Paris in 1869 with the fastest riders on 'Boneshakers'. The winner, though, was not a Frenchman but an Englishman, James Moore. Perhaps not a surprise, he had also won the first ever official cycling race the previous year in Saint-Cloud, Paris. Later, in the 1870s, he was also one of the first to purchase an Ariel, a fast Ordinary invented by James Starling. (An Ordinary? You know, one of those things that came to be nicknamed the Penny-Farthing. A. A. Milne referred to them as the 'dangerous'.)

After reaching our destination, we walked into Honfleur on the hunt for food and David's sudden craving for Pelforth beer (we'd enjoyed one on arrival in Biarritz some years before), but we didn't find one here, settling for a 'Grand biere, s'il vous plais' where you get what you're given, and you're given what you get. Honfleur's a nice place, by the way. Lots of restaurants, old buildings, cobbles, a harbour—but no Pelforth.

Day 4, 30th May, distance 127.82 kilometres (525.30 kilometres), elevation gain 929m (3,013m).

Depart: Honfleur. Arrive: Grandcamp-Maisy.

Weather: Sunny, 19 degrees, and a steady tailwind. Very blustery, occasionally buffeting us.

Food: Croissants, pain au chocolate, yoghurt, baguette, fruit, toasted veg sandwich, boiled egg, tuna rice salad, peanuts, fruit cocktail. (In other words, there is no room in the restaurant, so no dinner, just tea.)

Food was going to be an issue today. It started with David telling me at breakfast that he had picked a secluded place to sit in order to purloin a few snacks for lunch. When I took my place at the breakfast table, I could see that his choice was in direct line of sight of the reception, the bar, and the kitchens—a commando he does not make!

Passing the infamous beaches of the D-Day landings, we are where the events of D-Day, 6th June 1944 took place, arguably the most pivotal day in WW2 history.

Allied forces landed on beaches codenamed Utah Beach, Omaha Beach, Gold Beach, Juno Beach and Sword Beach in their courageous bid to liberate Europe. There are many amazing stories about the efforts of cyclists during WW2. We saw a plaque about Guillaume Mercader, a French cyclist and Resistance member who used his bike as a cover to send information to the Allies in the run-up to D-Day.

Being a member of the Fédération Français de Cyclisme, he was allowed by the Germans to ride his bike on training rides on the roads along the Normandy coast. However, he took notes on the German defences and produced detailed maps that the Resistance passed to the Allies to help the invasion. After the war, Mercader received the Croix de Guerre (cross of war) and, more importantly, continued racing.

We passed through Arromanches with the remainder of its Mulberry Harbour clear to see. If you haven't heard about these, they were portable but substantial prefabricated harbours that were taken across the English Channel to enable cargo to be rapidly and safely offloaded once the allied forces had successfully taken control of the beachheads.

We successfully stopped for a coffee in a pleasant café on the route. I say successfully because if you don't start looking early for a stop, the Sods law dictates that you'll have passed the last one on your route before you realise it. David was in a hurry to visit the facilities and requested, "…a large black coffee; I'm nipping to the toilet." Subsequently, whilst we were enjoying the break, our coffees arrived. A Grand Café Au Lait for Kate, me, and David's coffee.

"Where's my milk?"

"You asked for a large black."

"Yes, but I always have hot milk with it."

"So, you don't have black coffee, you want what Kate and I have got."

"So, what's that?"

"A large coffee that has milk in it."

Silent pause.

"Yes."

You've got to love him. Different world, alien language, but always brings a smile.

Before reaching our destination, we passed Pointe Du Hoc, a headland jutting into the sea where German guns were installed. There is now a monument here in memory of the allied forces. At this point, camouflaged army rangers, under fire, scaled the cliffs in the early hours of D-Day and took the post, which prevented the guns from bombarding the soldier-filled beaches of Omaha and Utah (good job David wasn't part of the team).

The sun was still shining, but it was very windy when the three of us walked into Grandcamp, passing the marvellously shiny world peace statue, which looked like a metallic heroine from a Marvel film. We were a little early, and having now learnt that French restaurants don't open until 7 p.m. we were allowing enough time to see what was available. Once we had realised that only one restaurant was going to open, we found a bar and enjoyed a beer whilst waiting for the opening time. We noticed, not for the first time on this trip, and certainly not the last, that people were wandering the streets with the same aim of finding sustenance. If we arrived at a restaurant at opening time, we could hope to get a table. There was a weakness in our plan, as relaxing with a beer is not conducive to arriving on time. We were almost ten minutes late, and the restaurant was full.

Dejected, we headed for the local supermarket, due to close in thirty minutes but only about 15 minutes away, knowing that if it closed, we'd have to resort to trying a roadside automated pizza-making machine. (Each secretly thinking that might be fun just to try it!) Wandering the aisles to find ourselves something to eat, we kept spotting the other zombie-like visitors who had also failed to get into a restaurant! The day ended with a fun-filled meal in our guest house, a large old farmhouse adjacent to grand, brick-built stables. The house had a lot of character, including a spiral staircase, old French furniture, and creaky floorboards. Around a table in our bedroom sat three cyclists, and on it were a baguette, 3 ready-made salads, a 1kg bag of salted peanuts, and 6 bottles of Pelforth beer. David was very happy!

Day 5, 31st May, distance 114.87 kilometres (640.17 kilometres), elevation gain 712m (3,725 kilometres) Depart: Grandcamp-Maisy. Arrive: Cherbourg.

Weather: Sunny but 40 kilometre-ish cross winds with 60 kilometre-ish gusts. Significantly buffeting us like a dog trying to gain attention.

Food: Pain au chocolate; croissant with ham and cheese; baguette; yoghurt; fruit; peanuts; an unpleasant chicken burger; lettuce; coleslaw; a pleasant cheesecake.

This is such a beautiful area, but it is scattered with reminders of battle, small war museums, memorials, bomb craters, and, lest we forget, war graves. Our ride included a stop to see a memorial for the French Resistance, where we also met a couple from Stratford-upon-Avon also riding a tandem. The French Resistance played a vital part in aiding the Allies, such as supplying them with intelligence and disrupting German supply lines. On June 18th, 1940, Charles de Gaulle addressed the people of France from London. He called on the French people to continue the fight against the Germans.

General Dwight Eisenhower said that in no previous war have the Resistance forces worked so closely with the military effort. The organised forces of the Resistance played a very considerable part in the final and complete victory. The statue included three characters: one man holding a gun, a woman manning a communication radio, and another man tying a message to a pigeon whilst leaning on his bike. They could have been David, Kate, and me.

We continued past the last of the D-Day beaches; Utah was the very last beach, and there was a memorial where a group of soldiers were paying their respects.

Where possible, I opted for roads away from the seafront today where we could have been blown off our bikes.

"The last thing I need now is a blow job," said David. "And that's the last thing that you'll be getting," commented Kate.

As we cycled along the coast, we stopped for lunch on a beach, sheltered from the wind next to a sea wall, where we could see the nearby island of Tatihou and the nearby fishing village of Saint-Vaast-la-Hougue. The village is famed for its oysters, and, at low tide, the oyster beds provide a link between the village and Tatihou Island (apparently, when the tide is low, you can walk across to the island). The Saint-Vaast-la-Hougue harbour is home to the Vauban de la Hougue tower, which stands at the entrance of the small harbour, and is a UNESCO World Heritage Site, along with its sister tower on Tatihou.

Then we arrived in Cherbourg, the final destination for David. No, he isn't dying just yet, but it's convenient for him to get the ferry back home from here. We had a pleasant walk on the seafront with views of the enormous harbour and then enjoyed an evening meal together. What is something that you wouldn't see on a walk through an airport terminal—perhaps stories of air disasters? Not so here. On the walk, we enjoyed reading stories to David presented on plaques along the sea wall about ferry disasters, ships that had sunk, and a whole collection of disasters at sea in and around Cherbourg! It was a little sad, though, that David would be leaving us, and it was nice to share the evening together, particularly if it's the last time we ever see him. The restaurant had limited options on the menu, and at first David was struggling to find something that he would like.

"Everything seems a bit spicy."

"Well, they've got a chilli burger, David."

"That would be a lot spicy?"

"Okay, how about Spag Bol."

"Could be a bit spicy, John."

"I'll go and see if you're allowed to order the breakfast cereal."

To finish the meal, I had an espresso, Kate had a cup of breakfast tea, and David requested Darjeeling with milk.

"You don't have milk in Darjeeling, David."

"I'm not in Darjeeling; I'm in Cherbourg."

Day 6, 1st June, distance 92.58 kilometres (732.75 kilometres), elevation gain 1,293m (5,018m).

Depart: Cherbourg. Arrive: Saint-Jean-de-la-Rivière (David, Chichester, UK).

Weather: Sunny spells, cross winds, occasional headwinds, and, if lucky, tailwind 30–50kph.

Food: Apple croissants, fruit cocktails, yoghurt, pain au chocolate, baguette, almonds, fruit consommé, boiled egg, sardines, crème caramel, peanuts, and dried fruit. (And the evening meal? There wasn't one.)

"Good luck catching the ferry, David, do you know the way?"

"No."

"Oh. Well, lots of good luck then."

Having given mutual good riddance, we got on our way.

After a lumpy throat (the D-Day beaches rather than David's departure), it was a bit of a lumpy route along this part of the coast today! It's not a surprise, really, when you are trying to keep to the coast. Possibly a rule that I could have added when planning the route is something along the lines of—if you can see it, you don't have to go down that way! ("Oo, look at that little rock down by the coast. Let's cycle and see what it is." 1 hour later; "Oo, it is a big rock.")

Anyway, it's too late for that. What can I say about this area? Heading first north-west (surely in the wrong direction) and then due south (see, no problem, and don't call me Shirley), the Cap de La Hague is a treat to cycle through, except on a windy day! We didn't need to suffer; we passed within a couple of kilometres of our return route from the headland! There was very little traffic on quiet country lanes, with quaint hamlets clinging to the tops of the seaside cliffs. Regular little fishing villages, attractive stone walls, and every now and then, a dramatic towering lighthouse or peaceful harbour.

Then there was the climb; we turned a corner, a sharp switchback, and I don't know where it came from, but we were in the wrong gear, staring at least 15%, perhaps more. I had to change gear quickly, but no, it was too late. The chain slipped over the biggest ring at the back, and we jerked to a halt.

This leads to a series of less-than-enjoyable experiences.

1. The instant split-second panic to grab the brakes, uncleat, and get a foot down onto terra firma, hopefully both choosing the same side to do this or we're going down with a bump. This includes trying to hold the tandem upright whilst we extricate ourselves and take some deep breaths whilst we shout, "Feck."
2. Inspecting the bike to work out what has happened. The chain is jammed behind the cassette (the collection of gears at the centre of the rear

wheel.) We can't move it with the luggage on, and even if we did, it could damage something. I can't release it without the potential of damaging the chain due to my immense strength. (I don't know why you find that funny.)
3. We are going to have to take all the luggage off, safely move the tandem somewhere (uphill) to remove the rear wheel, relocate the chain, and put it all back together again.

I set to work on sorting the jam out whilst Kate did a great job of disappearing down the hill, reappearing with the panniers, and going back for the rest. This wasn't the first time that we had been pleased with our decision to change from road shoes to MTB shoes for this trip; walking up and down that hill could have been a real challenge! We sorted it out but it reminded us how an obstacle can just be waiting around the corner. Now needing a rest and a drink, we also realised not to expect to find regular cafes around here; instead, another steep climb into the strong headwind, but we were ready for it. We realised what we needed to expect and anticipate on this section of coast and dug in.

There is a nuclear reprocessing plant in the area (Flamanville), which has a reputation for dumping radioactive waste and contaminating the local beaches. However, the weather was pleasant, the views lovely, and fantastic golden-glowing beaches, with locals that had apparently all had Ready Brek for breakfast, free central heating for everyone here! We seemed to pass surprisingly quickly through the terrain and arrived early, about 3.30 p.m., giving me some time to work on the tandem! Of course, we then failed to find anywhere to eat and had a 3 kilometres walk to a shop to get snacks for tea.

"What did you enjoy most today, David?"

"He's gone home," replied Kate.

I assume that's what Kate enjoyed most—the fact that he'd gone home, which was rather rude. That evening, David asked on our Facebook page: "Did you miss me," and I replied, "It was a tough day." (It would have been rude to say, "No.")

Day 7, 2nd June, distance 112.74 kilometres (845.49 kilometres), elevation gain 650m (5,668m).

Depart: Saint-Jean-de-la-Rivière. Arrive: Saint-Jean-Le-Thomas.

Weather: Some clouds until about 11 a.m., then sunny for the rest of the day. 30kph cross/tail wind.

Food: Baguettes, fruit consommé, crème caramel, bananas, dried fruit, peanuts, sardines, jelly sweets, pizza, cold meats, and pickled vegetables.

I woke with a warm glow this morning—mainly in the buttock area! But also with some excitement at the possibility of a distant glimpse of Mont Saint-Michel. Would that be a possibility? I had no idea; it was just most likely a hopeful thought that it might be seen in the distance. It might be around the corner, must be around the next corner, might be around the next bend, over the hill? Talking about the hill, we just had one long climb today. As we were about halfway through, we could hear two cyclists gaining on us and laughing and chatting loudly. It became evident that the woman was telling her partner that she could catch us before the top, and as she did, on her e-bike, she called back, "Wow, it's a tandem." She went on ahead. Her partner then noticed, as the hill levelled, that I had changed up a couple of gears. Laughing, he shouted, "Attention!" then burst into raucous laughter as we shot back past his partner, never to be seen again. Mind you, this was all in French, and I don't speak French (how do I know it was French then, je ne sais pas?)

As a child, my family swapped houses with a French family in Coutances, which we passed nearby. Coutances is twinned with Ilkley, where we lived, which I assume was no coincidence. Kate and I were in the same class at Ilkley Grammar School, Kate always says that I was the naughty boy, and she was the good girl; I can't argue. Twinning exists between towns in different countries to foster links between organisations and people, with the aim of encouraging international understanding and cooperation. Coutances is a similar size to Ilkley. The original twinning process began after the Second World War between the towns' secondary schools. As a result of these exchanges, the Council decided to twin with Coutances. Agreements were signed first by Ilkley and then by Coutances. Since then, there has been a lively programme of visits between Coutances and Ilkley, with many of the two towns' organisations taking part, and each year a civic visit takes place, with each town taking turns hosting the other. I wonder if it's just house swapping that goes on or whether husband/wife swapping is part of the deal.

Shortly after, we cycled through Granville, a place my family had been to on a day trip or two. I recall the French family had a Deux Chevaux (Citroen 2CV), which we borrowed because our car (a VW1600 fastback) was having trouble starting, but the exhaust fell off the 2CV on the way home. A bit like the early days of the Tour de France, we had to repair it ourselves. Unable to find a forge, we managed to put it back in place with some barbed wire from a fence! Granville, though, would I recall any of it? Why did we go there rather than straight to the closer beaches? By the way, when I say, 'swapped house', it was only for a couple of weeks of holiday, not permanent.

I'm not sure that I would have gotten my hands on any Calvados at that age (about 14), but it is something I answer in the affirmative if offered, as though I was weaned on it. This is an apple-growing area, and, on the road, there were signs for Calvados and Cidre. (Along with less enjoyable apple products.) Granville is also a fortified coastal town. So perhaps we went to Granville to a Calvados distillery (Brewery? Fermentation parlour?), the fortifications, or a big church. I wondered if I would recognise any of it. In fact, I did; I recognised the distinctive church—the overpowering Eglise Saint-Paul was instantly recognisable. So, we definitely went there, but would we go there just for a church? I wonder if there was a secret distillery in the catacombs.

The ride had gotten a little lumpy by now, with some short, sharp shocks up and down. But with only a few kilometres to go, we climbed up onto a cliffside, and there she was, C'est magnifique, in the middle of an enormous bay—the Mont-Saint-Michel. That was such an exciting moment. What a magnificent site. It did not disappoint, even from this distance, probably about 30 kilometres away, well, more than 10 kilometres anyway.

We stayed in a nice little town, Saint-Jean-Le-Thomas, and went for a nice walk to find a restaurant. The weather had become quite pleasant, and we also found a beach bar where we enjoyed a beer (lesson learnt, we had managed to reserve a table at a restaurant), the sunshine, and spectacular views across the bay, followed by a nice meal out. That's more like it!

Hands up for a moment; it's confession time. What did I say about testing your kit and knowing it all works before setting off on a tour? Well, a couple of issues have arisen, and it's important to get them sorted before they have more of an impact. The first is Kate's leg warmers; they're not staying up for more than 30 minutes. Oh, very funny. No, nothing to do with me. We were in the fortunate position of knowing that my cousin was joining us in a few days. Enough time to get some new leg warmers ordered for her to bring out, which she kindly did—and they were good quality Gore leg warmers that would prove worthwhile in the Pyrenees.

The other failure was our third 'large' bag that we had brought for jackets, gloves, spare parts, and so on, that lay across the panniers. It was a basic error and one that was bugging me. We always used a third, top-quality Ortlieb waterproof pannier, laid across the top of the two side panniers. This is what we used for our test rides as well. But a moment of stupidity (Kate, "Just the one?") led me to take a bag out of our cupboard that hadn't been used for at least 10 years. It didn't even look waterproof, with the tape hanging loose from the supposedly sealed seams and a sort of crackly feel to it. What was evident when checking its contents after the first light shower were damp cardboard boxes supposedly protecting spare chainsets, disc brakes, etc. We decided to watch out for our favourite French shop, Decathlon, and get a replacement. Only a few days later, we discovered one within 10 minutes' walk from our accommodation and came out with a fully waterproof, bright yellow bag that really did a great job when some nasty weather arrived. The sort of bag you might take on a kayak to keep things dry or possibly to catch air in and create a float in the event of being washed overboard on the ferry across the Loire.

<u>Day 8</u>, 3rd June, distance 122.98 kilometres (968.47 kilometres), elevation gain 763m (6,431m).

Depart: Saint-Jean-Le-Thomas. Arrive: Dinard.

Weather: Sunny, windy, 25kph cross tail wind most of the time, luckily!

Food: Baguettes, jam, yoghurt, fruit puree, bananas, peanuts, jelly sweets, salad, fish soup, pork belly and vegetables, chocolate pudding, and fruit.

After a slow start today, within a few kilometres we were confronted with a herd of sheep being steered down the lane towards us. We stopped and just waited for the sheep to brush past us. I was happy with the experience, but Kate was a little sheepish. You may have noticed that Kate and I don't talk a lot when we cycle. Well, it's not about cycling anyway, as we don't have any moans, we just love it. I guess the only exception is when she thinks she's the pilot. For the first few years after her accident, Kate was very compliant. She just got on the tandem, pedalled, and smiled. She had been a very good solo cyclist, club champion, and top ten in the CTT best all-rounder competition (Cycling Time Trials), Cycling Land's End to John O'Groats, and London-Paris-Geneva-Nice, for example. But she had never been good at technical downhills on climbs. (A straight downhill in a time trial seemed to be different, and I always put that down to adrenaline and competitiveness.) As I was the pilot, she suddenly accepted going much faster and was a natural at leaning into turns on the back. In the last few years, though, this has gradually changed. I don't know if I could cycle without her now, as I seem to be losing the ability to ride without her:

"Watch that car!"; "Wow, thanks, I hadn't noticed that."

"On the left!"; "Thanks, I was looking right, I'm glad you are here."

"Careful down here, it's a bit technical"; "Oh yes, I remember now when I plotted the route and thinking I hope I look out for this, thanks. I'm not sure we'd have gotten down here safely without you noticing, and I've got a book to write."

"I think the lorry is going to overtake."; "There's a lorry?"

"He's reversing out"; "Thanks, I had wondered what the lights on the back of the car were on for. I really need to retake my driver perception test now that I'm in my sixties."

(Of course, I'd rather she pointed things out in case I hadn't noticed.)

The year before last, we visited St Michael's Mount in Cornwall for the first time. Wading back across the causeway as the tide came in had been fun. Now we are here, next to Mont-Saint-Michel, Normandy, France. They look so similar and have the same name; what a coincidence!

Access to the Mont is either by walking or by shuttle bus (parking is at least a mile inland) or, it would seem, by horse and cart. This is all part of the efforts made to protect both the aesthetics of the island, but also the geography and ecosystems of the bay. Cycling up to the Mont is also permitted.

Much of the day was spent cycling around Mont-Saint-Michel Bay, which is between Brittany and the south-west, and along the Cotentin peninsula, Normandy, where we had cycled through. The bay is quite shallow, so when the tide is out, it empties and quickly refills when it comes in. Not much of a surprise, really.

The area around the bay has a complex series of roads and gravel tracks, making navigation a bit hit-and-miss. Sometimes you're on a good road, another time, a gravel or grass track. After a couple of backtracks, we eventually found our way through. We then found that Saint Malo was also tricky to navigate with only a few cycle paths that we came across, but the fortress-walled city looked impressive to visit another time. (It'd take at least a day to look around.)

Shortly after Saint Malo, we had an interesting crossing over the mouth of La Rance. Cycling over the Rance Tidal Power Station is not the easiest crossing. Retrospectively, it is perhaps expected that bikes stay on the main carriageway; however, it had two lanes with no bike lane or hard shoulder and was very busy. We decided to take the footpath, which was manageable but a bit fiddly, possibly intended for pedestrians. Once we had crossed, the main carriageway continued as two busy lanes up a hill, so we turned immediately up a lane on the right, which worked well, avoiding the traffic. But the crossing is rather special as it was the world's first tidal power station, opened in 1966, and with 24 turbines, it has achieved 0.12% of the power demand in France.

The use of tidal energy is not a new concept, as tidal mills have long existed in tidal areas. The potential of tides was taken advantage of by our mediaeval forbears, perhaps not enough so by us. Woodbridge Tidal Mill in Suffolk has been using tidal energy to mill grain for hundreds of years. Founded in 1170, it uses a dam to capture water when the tide is high. As the tide ebbs, the water is released through a sluice, which pushes a water wheel, which in turn activates the grinding stones.

The idea of constructing a tidal power plant in La Rance dates to the 1920s. The site was attractive because of the wide average range between low and high tide levels. Work did not commence until 1961 under the design and management of Albert Caquot, a visionary engineer. He created an enclosed area that would protect the construction site from the tides and the powerful ebb and flow of the river. Construction required draining the area, which required the construction of two dams and took two years. Construction of the power plant commenced on 20 July 1963, whilst the Rance was entirely blocked by the two dams.

Construction took three years and was completed in 1966. Charles de Gaulle, the President of France, inaugurated the power plant on 26 November of that year. The inauguration of the road crossing the plant took place on 1 July 1967, but what it overlooked, it would seem, was appropriate provision for cyclists. The actual connection of the plant to the French National Power Grid was carried out on my 6th birthday, 4 December 1967.

Our destination today was Dinard, and upon arriving at the hotel by about 3 p.m., it seemed like the hotel was not going to open for a while. No one was there, and we tried any door we could find, including trying a phone number on the bar that said when it would open. The bar eventually opened about half an hour late, but the barman was proving elusive. I attempted to hold a conversation with him, but he left me standing at the bar whilst he tinkered in the kitchen. Eventually he advised that he did not work in the hotel, that it was full, and that we'd need to speak to the manager who was also on his way.

About another half hour and the manager arrived. Again, he seemed to be too busy to hold a conversation with me and was dismissive when I suggested we had a room booked. Eventually, I was able to explain that we had a booking and had been waiting for 2 hours. He advised that he had taken charge of the hotel in April (we had booked in October), and he knew nothing of our booking. He said that he had been given no information by the previous owner. (Had no other guests turned up? Were we really the only ones booking between October and April?) It was time to leave, and when he realised, I was going, he said he had spare rooms, but the exchanges had not been friendly or apologetic, so we went to find a much nicer hotel with a restaurant overlooking a beautiful bay. We had some posh nosh and relaxed.

Day 9, 4th June, distance 99.99 kilometres (1,068.37 kilometres), elevation gain 1,354m (7,776m).

Depart: Dinard. Arrive: Hillion.

Weather: Sun all day, tail wind dropped to 15kph.

Food: Croissants, bread, sweet bread, jam, fruit cocktail, apples, baguettes, yoghurt, jelly sweets, pizza, nibbles.

Brittany is an area that we have not been to before, and we were quickly beginning to love it.

Almost every turn reveals something new. The bridge over the Frémur is a viaduct, and it hasn't been around all that long. In the 19th century, crossing the tidal estuary was possible by a ford at low tide. (I think a Citroen is more likely.) A wooden submersible walkway of about 25m was built in 1878 to enable people to cross, presumably when it wasn't submerged. Not really much of a crossing, is it?

"Where's the bridge?"

"Just there, under the water."

The first proper bridge over the Frémur was built of reinforced concrete and put into service in 1929 (did they have concrete then? I thought it was invented to build Stevenage New Town) but the bridge had a series of false starts over many years. Ultimately considered too narrow, the bridge was destroyed in 1979, but at least it had bridged a gap. It was replaced in 1980 by a straight reinforced concrete bridge.

It seems Brittany loves cyclists, courteous drivers, calls of encouragement, and even a professional cycling group passing opposite called out "Bravo." We were feeling very positive. At one point, an old road had been blocked off with earth piles, possibly to stop it from becoming a rat run. As we exited the road, an elderly Breton cyclist checked on the route with us, and we explained it was 'okay'. He had as much English as we had French. But we had a fun conversation, and he was interested in our goal. As he said farewell, he quickly explained that goodbye in Breton is 'Kenavo'. We called 'Kenavo' as we cycled away, and you could see that it pleased him.

After about 20 kilometres, we cycled past the Chateau de Beaussais, overlooking a sandy inlet, and looking across, we could see Saint-Jacut-de-la-Mer, so, decision, time! Do we cycle up the peninsula to its point, wasting a few kilometres to have to travel back down? Saint Jacut is on a peninsula between two sea inlets. The sandy beach slopes gently, which means at times you have a sandy bay and at other times the tide rushes in to provide a sea-filled bay. Did we cycle up? Well, what was the point?

Our destination for today is Hillion. Mussel farming is the main produce in this area, producing a significant amount—up to 10% of French mussels. We had great views of the mussel beds in the bays below, so I had no need to find a dead-end road today. Unsurprisingly, each year, a festival called 'La fete de la moule' is held in August on the mussel farm. Luckily, we will be long gone; if they discover a couple of snails in their midst, the mussel men might be less than impressed. In Hillion, we passed a moule restaurant—they served moules in every sauce you can imagine, c'est ça.

We expected a hilly day today, and, though it was, none were too steep, making it a little easier on the legs. At the top of one hill, a man with his wife called out something, and Kate called back, "Pardon, je suis anglaise."

"Ah, English, it is easier for two."

Kate called back, "That depends whether they are going uphill or downhill."

At our coffee stop today, a group of French teenagers sat in the corner, embroiled in conversation. The elderly waitress spoke no English but did her best to understand my order for two Grand Café au Laits. The French language is fun, like the word for big, the word grand. From a Grand Café au Lait (a little more than a double espresso with milk) via our favourite grand bier to the mountainous Grand Colombiere.

The waitress suddenly saw our tandem and became very vocal and excited. Rushing back to us, keen to say something, "En faisant du vélo ici sur votre tandem, vous avez apporté du beau temps avec vous, merci."

I turned to the teenagers and asked, "Does anyone speak English?"

"She is saying that whilst travelling on your tandem, you have brought the good weather with you. Thank you."

It was a lovely moment.

Kate almost died today. "I almost crashed to the ground, smashing my head on the concrete and spilling my brains, leaving my children and dog parentless." Occasionally, on a tandem, the stoker can overbalance in a gravitational vortex. (Well, this one can.) They are in suspended animation, leaning to one side and appearing as though they have lost the ability to just sit back up and regain balance. In the meantime, I, the pilot, use all the strength I have to stop the bike from falling over. This is how dangerous our lives are. Not far from death, infinitely closer to life, and if the worst should happen, the children would not be parentless as they'd have me. I have, however, not fathered a dog. Sorry, Phoenix, it's also time to tell you that she wasn't your real mum.

We arrived in a beautiful area today with enough time to go for a walk down to the local estuary, the Baie-de-Saint-Brieuc. Amazing for walks, there are beaches covered in shells, bird hides to sit quietly and spot the wildlife, idyllic bays with small fishing boats, and harbours. Brittany, what a place!

Day 10, 5th June, distance 69.76 kilometres (1,138.13 kilometres), elevation gain 1,002m (8,778m).

Depart: Hillion. Arrive: Paimpol.

Weather: some clouds, occasional sunny 20 but mainly clouds with 15kph cross-headwinds. (I tend to prefer a happy headwind.)

Today was a recovery day.

Food: Jelly sweets, peanuts, madeleine's, baguette, egg, salad, tuna baguette, fruit puree, roasted peanuts, bananas.

As we cycled out of Hillion, we realised that the Baie-de-Saint-Brieuc had even more to offer than we had time to see, sweeping along quiet roads past more beautiful towns and villages up and around the headland to our river crossing. Our route was blocked in Port de Legue by a turnstile bridge with the gates down, across, or whatever it is they do. Looking upstream a few kilometres away, I could see there was a modern towering viaduct with what appeared to be motorway vehicles crossing it. Do we just wait?

Kate spotted cyclists on the other side.

"There are cyclists waiting on the other side as well," she said. (Well, what do you expect her to say?). It was a hopeful sign. Within a couple of minutes, a van pulled up, and an 'operateur' (not promising, that's the official name, but one sometimes has a guess) got out and pressed some buttons in a nearby shed. Overexcited lights started flashing, and the platform swung into action, turning until its roadway provided a bridge for crossing. Then the barriers lifted, the flashing lights calmed themselves down, and over we went. We were lucky. I subsequently heard that just a few days later, a campervan, too high to be crossing here, damaged the crossing, and it had to be closed for a month!

Sadly, that was the excitement done for the day. We spent much of the day cycling out of view of the sea and often between hedges. Then we arrived at an exceedingly forgettable port known as 'the beauty spot of the Côtes d'Armor'. Port de Binic is described as a quaint fishing and sailing village. We stopped for a coffee but really weren't impressed. Just an average place with carparks and garish restaurants. Of course, if the Cotes d'Armor only consists of Binic, then perhaps it is the local beauty spot—sometimes you have to make do, don't you?

"Yes, you do!" agreed Kate.

Today was our least favourite so far. However, we did notice, and it was good to see a number of female cycle tourers riding solo (something positive to say!) and did so throughout the holiday.

With Paimpol almost in sight today, we approached a fast downhill bend, and I could see that just past it there was a sharp right-hand turn, which we took and immediately plunged steeply downhill for about 700 metres or so before coming to a pebbled cove, 'Boulgef' looking out across mussel beds.

"It's a dead end," Kate said.

"I know, but mussel farming is an important part of this area, and I wanted to get a photo of the exposed mussel beds."

Photo taken.

Kate said, "There was an identical right turn about 25 metres further along the road."

"I know, but this was a good photo opportunity."

"You went wrong, didn't you?"

"Yes."

We now had today's 'cheeky little climb' to do.

Paimpol is a tourist destination in Brittany, so a shorter recovery ride was planned to enable us to check out the renowned beaches and the port of Paimpol. Was it worth it? No, not really. (Perhaps it was just a mood thing today.) The port is pleasant, and the old town next to the marina has cobbled streets filled with restaurants, cafés, and bars. Just the sort of place tourists can enjoy looking around and having a drink and a good meal. It didn't really look like a good holiday base, but with bays, peninsulas, and coves to explore, it's possibly not a bad place to pass through. A beer and something to eat were all we needed! Unfortunately, it was a no-alcohol day.

"Ah, that's the problem," Kate said.

On arrival in Paimpol, we needed to turn into the driveway to our accommodation but had another challenging situation to deal with. A gang of local hoodies barred our way. I looked and smiled, in what felt like a kind of paedophilic manner. (I hasten to add, 'Not that I'd know') But there was no reaction. I quickly made a plan of action. 'Take my beautiful wife; do as you will with her, but please give her back. I have nursed her back from trauma before, and I'm sure I can do so again—but only if I am fit and healthy to do so'. Luckily, they realised where we were going and kindly moved on. I still can't believe that parents allow seven-year-olds to go out on their bikes by themselves. Mind you, that was normal when I was that age.

Day 11, 6th June, distance 90.14 kilometres (1,228.27 kilometres), elevation gain 1,299m (10,077m).

Depart: Paimpol. Arrive: Ploumanac'h.

Weather: overcast and nippy until 2 p.m. Glorious day by 4 p.m. (okay, evening).

Food: Bread, jam, baguettes, emmental, apples, peanuts, fish pate, toast, sardines, mashed potatoes, Breton tart with figs.

In, out, up, and down (to be honest, we've already had quite a lot of this, and I don't mean early morning Pilates.) Most days for the last week have been windy and overcast until about 2 p.m. So typically, it's been bib shorts, long-sleeve base layer, and gillet…with the gillet removed when the sun comes out and stays out. This is Brittany, so I soon realised that yesterday's disappointment was just a blip.

Sillon de Talbert is a geological phenomenon that's worth seeing if you are in the area and is great for walking, I would think. It's a long, thin trail of pebbles stretching far into the sea. Recalling the extremes of weather that we are getting from the Global Warming Company, when I saw it, my first thought was, *Well, that won't be there this time next year*. It's a thin line of land reaching a few kilometres into the sea that is only about 30–40 metres wide and is made up mostly of sand and pebbles—just look at it on a map; it's fascinating. It's situated between two estuaries, and apparently the tidal currents of the two rivers have created this incredible phenomenon. I managed to take some photos, but really showing what it looks like would probably take an aerial shot. (Which sounds like a sniper taking aim at a Disney mermaid.)

We found a café stop—a typical bar/tabac that had a group of locals enjoying their favourite tipple. Whilst we sipped our coffee and devoured a baguette and a bar of emmental, the locals seemed interested to hear about our endeavour. The landlady's English was good enough to assist with the translation, but as we got up to leave, the landlady wished us 'bon voyage' and 'enjoy your stay in France'. One local immediately said (in Breton) that we are not in France; we are in Brittany! We laughed, but it was another reminder of the pride of the Bretons. The main language of Brittany is French, but the traditional language of Breton (Brezhoneg) is much older and has similarities to the Welsh and Cornish languages. Although Brittany and the Bretons are part of France, many Bretons do not perceive themselves as being French but rather as a separate Celtic people in France.

Hey, let's go find a lighthouse! Phare de Nantouar is very quaint. What the fascination is with lighthouses, I have no idea. No, it's not just me; it's a tourist thing. Built in 1860, the Nantouar lighthouse is located on the harbour of Perros-Guirec, near today's destination. There was no sign of any fire damage, but I did read that the lighthouse was extinguished in 1976.

This is the reason for cycle touring and discovering places like this. Cycling around here is stupendous—scenic coastal roads and fine sandy beaches either covered in pebbles or scattered with rose granite rocks. Yes, it's hilly, but most hills max out at 1 kilometre and barely get above about 6 percent. (There were two that went into double figures but only for a short stretch.)

Finally, today, Plage Saint-Guirec is picturesque, sandy, and surrounded by the pink granite of the region, which is so attractive. There are various small sandy coves along the coast, and the harbour is also very pleasant to walk around. What is it with place names that end with 'h' around here? They are very common, and I assume it has something to do with the Breton language, specifically the pronunciation of the name, but I couldn't find out.

Day 12, 7th June, distance 91.30 kilometres (1,319.57 kilometres), elevation gain 1188m (11,195m).

Depart: Ploumanac'h. Arrive: Morlaix.

Weather: Cloudy with light tailwind. Sunny from 1 p.m., nice for cycling.

Food: Bananas, bread, emmental, pain au chocolate, peanuts, cereal bar, goat cheese salad, chicken chorizo, frites.

The route was similarly hilly today, but the climbs got a little steeper (15%) and a couple touched 20%, whilst Brittany just got nicer and nicer. Over the last couple of weeks, we have had to take detours to avoid road works or gravel tracks, which in some ways is annoying but also adds to the challenge and excitement.

Our destination today is the town of Morlaix, where I have booked us in for 2 nights to give us a rest day and domino break. It's inland (south) to enable us to get over a cycle-friendly river bridge. But there are places you sometimes arrive at that make you wonder why you've never heard of them before. Morlaix has an attractive port with tall, grand houses lining each side. It appeared very popular, not unpleasantly so, with what I guess is referred to as pleasure craft. (Though the phrase 'pleasure craft' does sound more like either a strong beer or a 'professional' occupation to me.) It's a great place for people-watching.

"Did you say domino break?" Queried Justine.

"I did so."

"Oh, okay."

"I told you he'd think that was a silly question," whispered Stuart.

"Unless it's just the first of a series of very subtle, clever questions, my love."

But there's another side to the town, which is dissected by a dominating and magnificent viaduct (I do love a bridge) with 14 arches, built in the 19th century using local granite to enable trains to travel between Brest (yes, I had to correct the spell checker) and Rennes.

Beyond the viaduct, where we were staying, are old mediaeval houses and narrow streets to explore.

Next to the viaduct there's a stairway to heaven, well, to a 15th-century church, Saint-Mélaine, and behind it steps continue up to reach a viewpoint across the town of Morlaix. (Rather than my delightful description of the place, I could have just given this information and said, nice place, go see for yourself! Come to think about it, rather than putting in all this effort to write a book I could have just posted on Facebook—done it, now you do it, lots to see.) It is free to walk across the viaduct (lower level—the top is for trains) and well worth it.

The mediaeval houses are worth seeing on Rue Ange de Guernisac and in Place des Otages's 16th century town houses.

Sad to note though, amongst many of the Nazi scars you come across in France, the Place des Otages refers to hostages who were brought here on 26 December 1943 before being deported to Nazi concentration camps.

Mediaeval houses vary greatly with the timbered structure you'd expect to see, but some carry carvings, others are painted colourfully, and some have tiled facades.

One of the houses on Place Allende, just up the road from our accommodation, can be visited for a few francs (sorry, for one second, an unexpected and little-known impact of Brexit was that the French had reverted to the franc, perhaps to confuse the English when they arrive on holiday with their euros) and is a 'Lantern House' called the 'Maison de la Duchesse Anne'. It dates from the early 16th century. The 'lantern' refers to an interior courtyard in the house that contains a fireplace and a staircase to the upper stories and allows light to enter the building. Worth going out of your way for; it's amazing. My favourite part was a u-shaped gutter that led rainwater in from the back of the house, under the staircase, and back out at the front of the house.

On a hill near the Place Allende, you can reach the site of the ancient castle by following the 'escaliers du château'. Don't get too excited though (we didn't), as there hasn't been a castle there since the 1500s—Kate thought it provided very nice views, unobstructed by castle walls.

Dominoes can be stood on one end, side by side, in trails, forming different patterns and shapes. You then give the first one a tap, and it falls, hitting the next one, then the next, and so on. If you leave a few gaps, then you won't knock them all over by accident; just a few, you know this. Likewise, if you have a couple of days of regular rest on a tour, if something goes wrong, it can allow you to catch up without having a knock-on for the whole tour like dominoes. Kate and I didn't feel we needed a rest, but it did give us time to look around Morlaix properly and spend some time with Justine and Stuart.

Day 13, 9th June, distance 101.76 kilometres (1,421.33 kilometres) elevation gain 1,259m (12,454m).

Depart: Morlaix. Arrive: Kermarguel.

Weather: Light rain am, mild but overcast pm, light tailwind. Doesn't really feel like summer, but pleasant enough.

Food: Bananas, apple puree, toast and honey, banana, ½ tuna baguette, ½ chocolate baguette, oysters, venison, vegetables.

Back on the road then (well, we were getting bored) and joined by cousin Justine and her husband Stuart for a couple of days. (Ah, now I understand.) They joined us for a day a few years ago when we cycled from John O'Groats to Margate via Land's End. Although Justine tends to ask silly questions, we were impressed with how they rode. We may have to up our speed for a couple of days, perhaps wearing earplugs. (For their newly discovered aerodynamic properties.)

Cycling north from Morlaix takes you along the estuary as it opens to the sea. Dotted here and there are little islands, including an outcrop with a castle on it (Chateau du Taureau); the Ile Louet with a lighthouse, a cottage, and a cove with a causeway leading out to another island; and the Ile Callot with some houses and a church. It's all so tempting to stare at when you need to keep half an eye on the road!

"How do you keep half-an-eye on the road?"

"I don't need to. I sit on the back of a tandem and keep half an eye on the view," answered Kate.

Toilet breaks: Let's get down to the nitty-gritty…well, hopefully not gritty, but how they work. If you are a walker, runner, or cyclist, there will be times when you need to go. It can happen, but not that often, that this coincides with a coffee stop or an unlocked public toilet, but usually requires at the very least a quiet road and a fig leaf! We look out for a suitable stop, pull over, and if one of us needs to pop behind the hedge, then, when they return to hold the tandem, the other will usually attempt to go as well to reduce the number of potential stops!

Kate had requested a toilet stop, and I spotted a suitable location, announcing, "Stopping," and applying the brakes. Unfortunately, for Justine, she had just taken her bidon out for a drink and drinking with one hand whilst braking with the other is not likely to go well. In panic, she gave a little yelp and just tossed the bidon away to brake safely! A very funny image. This squeaky little yelp is something that we would hear again a few times on the journey! A little forlorn look from Stuart and a knowing nod of the head kind of said, "Yep, this is normal." "Tossed the Bidon"—blimey, that's some sort of euphemism!

Shortly after this stop, I could hear a loud bird-like sound ahead. It was unfamiliar and unusually loud. As we got close to a corner, there was a small stream gushing and gurgling through a stone trough beside the hedge, and there was a large frog making the noises. The frog looked to jump into the water out of sight, so I carried on past, but Stuart pulled up to find a second, smaller frog croaking loudly. It also quickly jumped in but then blew out its cheeks, almost like blowing a large bubble-gum bubble. It's the sort of thing you see in wildlife films, but nothing any of us have seen live before.

Then we arrived at Roscoff, out on a peninsula surrounded by the sea. (All right, just on three sides.) A small, attractive town with houses that once belonged to pirates, a Gothic-style church, and a delightful seashore resort. Attractive seems to me to be a strange adjective for a town, and Roscoff, being described as a 'sexually alluring town', could well allure the wrong type of tourist.

We passed a number of coastal nature reserves today, but the Baye Kernic stood out as of particular interest. The bay is a stopover for migratory birds such as spoonbills, egrets, shelducks, sandpipers, curlews, ring-necked plover all taking advantage of this area for some rest and recuperation. It was great to see the egrets; I can't recall seeing them in the wild before. They're either a type of heron or just little toddler herons, and they sound like baby pterodactyls, maybe. Plant life is just as diverse, with species such as the pyramidal orchid, bindweed and the glasswort; along with the turquoise colour of its waters, it gives the appearance of a distant and exotic destination.

Today's destination is beside a river, Le Quillimadec, with the mouth of the river entering yet another picturesque bay with sun-lit waters, reeds, long grasses, boulders the size of houses, and sandy beaches all so nice.

Our accommodation was particularly nice this evening, and the hosts were very welcoming, interested in our venture, and very friendly. The apartment was also particularly pleasant, with a self-contained corridor, plush bathroom, lounge area with a beer (can't go wrong there), and a comfy separate bedroom. This had black-out blinds for a good night's sleep, unless you needed the toilet!

Kate awoke at night, and there was no emergency lighting plan in place. I could hear her moving towards the door but could not see her. Then there was a thud and, 'shit'. Moments later, from a different direction, another thud, 'shit', then a third thud and 'shit'.

I decided to get up, move straight to the door, and open it to provide some light for her; it was literally pitch black. Unfortunately, before reaching the door, I bumped into Kate, which resulted in us both mumbling 'shit' at the same time. I manoeuvred Kate out of the way and whispered, "Don't move," but without realising it I was now disoriented and walked straight into a wall, 'shit', then banged my head on a sloping ceiling, 'shit' and I was now back where I'd started.

By this time, we were both sniggering and snorting, trying not to laugh out loud. Kate warned that she was going to wet herself. I said that I now knew where I was.

"I'll try to get to the door again, try not to get in my way."

"Okay," she whispered, making me almost shit myself as she was back in bed next to me and had said that right in my ear. I got out of bed, edged along it to the foot, then took a few steps diagonally across the room, bumping into the door at first attempt. "Shit" (I could hear Kate giggling in bed.) I then felt around until I found the doorknob and opened the door, and there it was—the light at the end of the tunnel. I could now go back to bed and enjoy a nice, dry sleep.

Day 14, 10th June, distance 105.52 kilometres (1,526.85 kilometres), elevation gain 1,259m (13,713m).

Depart: Kermarguel. Arrive: Le Conquet.

Weather: 15kph headwind, sunny, enjoying retirement.

Food: Fruit pancake with honey, croissant with prune jam, pate, bread, nuts, burger and fries (shared), fish soup, sardine, and tuna pizza. The best breakfast so far and remained so for the rest of the trip, thanks 'Ker Bel Leur'—though some came close, and most were good.

Part way through the cycle today we had another Justine-ism whilst climbing a short but steep hill. Justine chose to ride up beside us in the middle of the road just as a car came down, so with an 'oh!' (Similar to the squeaky little yelp she gave when she discarded her bidon yesterday!) she turns off across the road into someone's driveway! Without hesitation, did a loop in front of their property before re-emerging to drop in behind us all. She acts as though this is perfectly natural, and no one will comment. We don't; we just drop our gaze and silently shake our heads. Noisily shaking our heads would be alarming.

The cycling around here is gorgeous. Our route has been heading towards the Île Vierge lighthouse, and I pick up that Stuart and Justine have both spotted it in the distance and are hoping we ride near it. For a while, it looked like the route I had planned would miss it, but it reappeared again and is now quite close. We cycle down the road, and a beautiful site begins to open up as we get closer. At first, we can see the lighthouse in the distance and sand dunes in the foreground. As we approach, we can then see a bay with boats expanding out before us, and finally, a cosy little sandy beach fills in the final detail, picture perfect.

Today we cycled around two large tidal estuaries, travelling several kilometres inland to find bridge crossings. The second of these estuaries was the Aber Benoît, which winds through parks and forests. A nice-looking place to walk. When the tide is low, mudflats appear, and this is another mussel-growing area, also known for its oysters.

Le Conquet is the westernmost town on the French mainland (though I did have to keep zooming in and out on the map, almost banging my head on the table, to check this, so it must be a closely run contest!) it's a busy fishing and sailing port. Apparently, Henry Tudor landed here blown off course when he fled from Wales: "Dost thou think I would *choose* to venture ashore in as god-forsaken place as this!" (Stuart does have a strange accent.)

The final part of our ride today took us out onto a headland opposite our destination, rather than inland to cross a bridge. On the way, I had spotted a footbridge across from one side to the other, I was relieved to find that it existed (the Passerelle du Croae) because it seemed an unusual place for a footbridge, and it was a fun route to end the day.

Day 15, 11th June, distance 77.48 kilometres (1,604.33 kilometres), elevation gain 1,200m (14,913m).

Depart: Le Conquet. Arrive: Irvillac.

Weather: Sunny, 21 degrees with a "Summer breeze, makes me feel fine…"

Food: Apple tarts, figs, almonds, salad, apricot tartlets, prune bread, jelly sweets, hot chicken roll.

"Bye-bye, Justine, bye Stuart." For breakfast, we found a coffee shop that also sold tart au pomme (Breton style). We enjoyed this before setting off in different directions.

Justine and Stuart realised they'd left their car at Morlaix and left us to head back, cross-country, to reclaim it. (The third side of a triangle, sort of.) They had quite a long ride to fit in, whilst I'd sneaked in a shorter ride today, hoping they wouldn't find out. (That didn't work John, did it? Why not? It was very hilly wasn't it—and the hills were steeper, weren't they? Yes, they were, my preciousss.)

Leaving Le Conquet and on the way to Brest, we saw some interesting sights. Within a few kilometres, as the road curved around the peninsula, we passed a lighthouse that appeared to protrude through an ancient building, providing a stunning juxtaposition; this was the Pointe Saint-Mathieu. Nestled on top of the cliffs are a small group of houses in the shadow of the ruins of the Abbaye Saint-

Mathieu de Fine-Terre. The merchants of Léon, according to legend, were saved from drowning off this headland as they brought back the body of the Apostle Matthew. The first monastery was founded here by Tanguy in the 6th century to house Saint Matthew's relics and was said to have held the skull of the apostle, now lost in the ocean off the pointe.

The Abbaye had many money-making powers, including, in 1157, having been granted by Herve de Leon, the right to flotsam and jetsam from wrecks; in 1390, it gained the right to a percentage of the wrecks of ships and their cargo and subsequently the right to the remains of those who perish at sea on these coasts. Don't you just feel you need some more information to contextualise these privileges? The 'modern' lighthouse was built in 1835, no doubt at great annoyance to the monks, or were they pirates, whose livelihood relied on the ships hitting the obstacles around the coast?

Up ahead along the coast, we could see a commanding German blockhouse that looked out across the horizon. It appeared to have glazed windows and was evidently being used for some other purpose. As we passed nearby, a sign said it was the Musee Memoires 39–45. The museum focused on telling the story of the war in Brittany through the personal accounts and anecdotes of those who lived through it. The roads are so smooth around here, and the tandem is gliding nicely along. Cycling is so easy and enjoyable.

And then, upon reaching Brest, we found the amazing castle walls. Brest is a large city, almost totally destroyed towards the end of World War II. It was rebuilt with just its castle and the Tanguy Tower surviving alongside just a few other buildings. Brest remains an important harbour and military port, second only to Toulon in the Mediterranean.

On leaving Brest, we begin to look for the bridge over L'Elorn because the tandem gets even heavier in water. When I first looked at this crossing, I could see that a bridge over L'Elorn carried what was likely to be busy N165 traffic—did it even have a cycle way across it? I then spotted a parallel bridge next to it, which brought a smile to my face. A parallel bridge is nearly always a foot or cycle bridge.

The Albert-Louppe Bridge is an arch bridge that stretches about 1 kilometre across the mouth of the Elorn River. Construction was completed in 1930, but the bridge was partly destroyed by the German army in 1944, and shortly after, it was closed for repair and reopened after widening and construction five years later. Between 1991 and 1994, another bridge, the Pont de l'Iroise, was built parallel to this bridge, leaving the Pont Albert Louppe perfect for farm vehicles, pedestrians, and cycling. The Paris-Brest-Paris cycle event used the bridge as a landmark. It is one of the oldest races in existence, starting in 1891. (The year I think I recall that Cycling Weekly was first published.) Although it was last raced professionally in 1951, it continues as an amateur event that runs every four years or so in the style of an audax or brevet, where you stop at points on the way to get proof you've completed the course.

As I mentioned, this was a tough day to Irvillac, with long drags and steep 15% climbs.

Grinding up a long 2.5-kilometre drag, at one point the road kicked up and we were almost grinding to a halt. "Sacré bleu!" All of a sudden, the bike picked up speed quite quickly, and it seemed at first that Kate had very smoothly and powerfully accelerated. But I soon realised that a French runner, now shouting 'Allez, Allez' had run up behind us and was pushing us along. He managed probably about 20–30 metres before calling out something like 'Bon Voyage' as the road became less steep, and we got our speed up whilst laughing and calling out our thanks. More road closures today, detours, and poor roads are so slow even downhill. It was such a relief to arrive in town just after 3 p.m. to give us a chance to look around. We found ourselves with little food on a Sunday. Not a good idea in France unless you're in a holiday resort. Luckily, though, we found a hot sandwich shop that opened for 3 hours in the evening, phew! (The sandwich was hot, not the shop, but it was delicious, err, the sandwich.)

Data ran out on my phone today (another negative consequence of Brexit is the limits on data roaming) on the very evening we don't have Wi-Fi. I spent most of the evening trying to add data until I recalled that I could tether to Kate's phone to post the day's story to Facebook, but it was getting quite late, and a few followers had by then sent messages to check that all was well, which was really comforting and appreciated.

Day 16, 12th June, distance 121.41 kilometres (1,725.74 kilometres), elevation gain 1,793m (16,706m).

Depart: Irvillac. Arrive: Douarnenez.

Weather: light wind. Overcast in the morning, sunny by 2 p.m., becoming a bit of a pattern.

Food: Fruit loaf, prunes, ½ chicken baguette (we shared one), almonds, chorizo and egg crepe, sardine crepe with salad, grain bar, and a few sweet chews.

What was I thinking when I planned today's ride? It felt just a bit long, with quite a lot of tough little climbs! Still, we've only been cycling for 2 ½ weeks, so bags of energy!

We had another very welcome bridge, this time over the Aulne, and it was yet another stunning crossing, this time with a very good, designated cycle path across it. We then passed Saint Nic today, but after a few kilometres, I decided to double back, and I took the opportunity to give him a letter on his naughty list that explained that it was all just a misunderstanding. Here we also passed a beautiful, 4-kilometres-long beach that extends from Saint-Michel-en-Grève to Saint-Efflam. It was beautiful for walking and enjoying the setting sun, but warning signs suggested it might not be so good for swimming due to problematic green algae. No worries; Spiderman has been contacted, "With great power comes great responsibility; I must defeat the problematic Green Algae." "I think that was the Green Lantern," said Kate.

It was at about this point that I looked at the 'distance to go' on my Garmin, and something didn't look right—somewhere we had lost about 40 kilometres—how can that be possible? (Do you put a question mark if it's a rhetorical question?).

"Kate, something's wrong; we've lost about 40 kilometres."

"How can that be possible?" (Told you)

"I have no idea; we need to stop and check."

When you follow a planned route on Garmin, it can let you know how far there is to go to your destination. For some reason, we only had about 20 kilometres to go when I would have expected about 60 kilometres to go. It was going to be a very short day. I looked at the route to see if anything looked wrong, and we appeared to have missed out on a peninsula! We thought back over the ride that we had done, and there had been several detours off our route during the morning. There had been an unpaved road where, to avoid it we had taken a detour and rejoined our route, and also a couple of closed roads due to road works where we had also followed deviations until being able to rejoin the planned route. (Something we seem to have had to do a few times each day.)

We then recalled one long deviation where it had taken a long time to be able to rejoin our route. I recalled zooming out on the Garmin at one point and seeing that it would cross our path if we stayed on our present route—what I hadn't realised was that we were cutting across to our return journey from the peninsula. (Which was closer.) Once we met it, we followed it and cycled for about another

5 kilometres before I registered that the distance to our destination was a bit short!

"Well, we will have to go back then and continue up the headland in reverse," said Kate.

So we did. We cycled the 5 kilometres back to where we had joined what should have been our return journey (and would be again in a couple of hours) and did a loop of the peninsula, then back to St Nic. (As I've already mentioned.) How did we cope with that? It's interesting; at the time, there didn't seem to be any disappointment or frustration; any blame; we didn't discuss a decision, and we weren't daunted by the additional cycling we'd have to do. We turned the tandem around and set off, knowing that we needed to avoid going back to the point where the roads were closed but at least going back up the peninsula. Looking back on this, I think it has something to do with our attitude: "Bottom line: you have to expect the unexpected and be okay with it." (Kyle Macrae, The Mental Cyclist) It's simple, but that seems to be it.

We just had the remainder of the ride on to Douarnenez, which turns out to be a pleasant town on the coast with several harbours. A lovely place for a stopover with narrow streets, busy harbours, bars, and craft shops. Our long evening walk into the town provided great views over the bay and of the harbour, as well as a Roman salt fish factory. This dates from the second century and is apparently the largest known of its kind. (There are others?)

Nearby, there was also a 'lavoire', a French communal wash house. You see these in almost every village around France, and this one was used up until about 1960.

In town, we went to our first creperie. All these years coming to France, and this was our first. It wasn't our favourite meal, but it was worth the experience and quite unusual, with chorizo and egg crepe as a starter and a fish crepe salad for the main. (Or was that the other way round?) I imagine at least one of them isn't classified as a crepe, perhaps a galette, which may or may not be the savoury version…all these things to learn, it's great. Also, what do you have as an entrée in a creperie? Another crepe—well, they didn't question it when I ordered!

Day 17, 13th June, distance 129.52 kilometres (1,855.26 kilometres), elevation gain 1,318m (18,024m).

Depart: Douarnenez. Arrive: Benodet.

Weather: Sunny, 24 degrees, light crosswind. For a summer holiday, the weather has not been great, but in a way it's quite good for cycling.

Food: Baguettes, croissants, fruit cocktails, Breton cake, baguette, salmon pate, fig rolls, sea snails, shrimps, oysters, cod, vegetables, mini desserts (Café Gourmand.)

The morning is hilly, though apart from one bump, they are less steep today. Nonetheless, they drag on a bit as the day heats up. 'Drag' sounds negative; it isn't really; it's just a fact and means we are slower, but we've allowed for slower, so all is good. Coming down one hill at about 50 kph the front brake makes an awful grating clatter as we approach a corner, and although I released the brakes, the noise continued, never exactly reassuring that type of thing. After inspection, we decided to change the front disc brake pad, and whilst doing so, I discovered a piece of metal fused to the disc. It appears that the sprung brake pad holder has become very hot whilst braking and has welded itself to the disc. A few knocks with the screwdriver attachment, and it breaks free, phew! The brake is sorted—but what is it with quick DIY jobs…it's taken about 45 minutes. I've been known to put up a shelf, allowing myself half an hour and taking three or four (weeks).

Aiming for a bridge across Le Goyen, we cycle through Audierne. Historically a fishing village, the harbour is now filled with yachts and pleasure craft faced by shops, restaurants, and bars. "Shall we have a break?" The brakes are very reassuring now.

The area has its own WW2 story with the battle of Audierne Bay, which took place at the end of the war. Allied warships were in control of the area off the coast of Brittany and engaged with German forces in the port of Brest when they intercepted and sank eight German vessels as part of what was codenamed Operation Kinetic. Kinetic was an allied operation aimed at intercepting shipping and hindering German forces besieged at Brest, consequently freeing us to cycle over the bridge at Audierne.

We also passed close to the Grotte de Menez Dregan. We didn't have the time to stop, but apparently this was a marine cave that has been partly protected due to the collapse of its 'roof', protecting the site from erosion. Evidence shows that the cave may have been inhabited prior to the Neanderthals, possibly 465,000 years ago. Then (the stories keep coming around here) only a few kilometres further, on the coast near Plozevet, we passed a monolith called the Menhir des Droits de l'Homme (in French). This is a large menhir erected in 1840 to commemorate the shipwreck of the 'Droits de l'Homme' (which seems to translate as the 'Rights of Man') in 1797, with the loss of around 600 lives. The menhir is engraved (in French), and translated approximately as follows:

Here, around this druidic stone, are buried about 600 shipwrecked of the ship 'Human Rights', shattered by the storm on January 14, 1797. Major Pipon, born in Jersey, miraculously escaped this disaster, returned to this beach on July 21, 1840, and was duly authorised, having engraved on the stone this lasting witness of his recognition. (Pipon was one of twenty-five survivors out of the one thousand two hundred on board.)

The approach to Benodet was over a bridge, and there were signs directing cyclists to a small cycle path leading onto the path that takes you over it. Crossing the bridge, I was disappointed that we had followed the signs, as the road was narrow and we'd have had a queue of happy and patient motorists behind us all the way across if we'd remained on the road. Additionally, the cycle path was raised with what felt like a perilously high kerb to our left. The width of the path was fine, but it felt very precarious, and it was a relief to arrive in Benodet.

Day 18, 14th June, distance 110.60 kilometres (1,965.86 kilometres), elevation gain 1,145m (19,169m).

Depart: Benodet. Arrive: Lorient.

Weather: Sunny, 24 degrees, 15 kph crosswind is only slightly annoying.

Food: Baguettes, fruit salad, boiled egg, fruit loaf, yoghurt, croissant, apple, banana, fig rolls, niçoise pizza.

Hey, guess what? We're going for a bike ride. Cycling through Concarneau was a nice surprise. This is a harbour town, and as we passed the harbour, we came across a stone bridge leading over into the original fortified town standing on an island in the harbour. Entering through the ramparts, there are delightful narrow streets, what appeared to be a walk around the walls themselves, restaurants, and gift shops. It was a bit early, in the day but a coffee stop was a good excuse. I wish I'd chosen this as a stopover, but the things we are seeing by avoiding direct routes from A to B are stunning.

We had some other delightful places that we passed through today, such as Pont-Aven in order to find a bridge over the Aven (spoilt for choice on that task); the artist Gauguin had once lived here; the Pont de Saint-Maurice (also to cross a bridge); along the coast we passed beach after beach; and finally, up the Blavet estuary. The riding is easy and fun, and we both feel extremely relaxed at this time. For lunch, we sat on a wall next to a picturesque mill, the Moulin a Marée du Henan. Built in the 15th century by Jean de Cornouaille, the tidal mill is positioned on a small old bridge across an estuary and works thanks to the ebb and flow of the tide on the river, ahead of its time. Today had been undulating but tandem or tourer-friendly, so we did arrive earlier than usual. On the map, this looked like a tricky area to pass through, so we didn't; we stopped in Lorient. I was also expecting it to be industrialised, but it turned out to be modern but nice, with lots to see.

Our accommodation was close to a wartime submarine base, and we took the opportunity to visit it. After the fall of France in June 1940, Karl Dönitz, in charge of the U-boats, was keen to use the French ports on this coast as bases for the German submarines. Prior to this, the U-boats had to travel from ports in Germany, so this relocation meant that the U-boats could be more effectively deployed. Already a French naval base, Lorient had the facilities Dönitz needed, and he immediately set to work on building the base at Lorient. Subsequently, the other bases were built along the 'Atlantic Wall', and we were to pass these on our journey over the next few days.

Day 19, 15th June, distance 101.18 kilometres (2,067.04), elevation gain 773m (19,942m).

Depart: Lorient. Arrive: Vannes.

Weather: Sunny, 24 degrees, 10kph tailwind helping us bob-a-long.

Food: Baguettes, yoghurt, croissant, egg, chewy sweets, pain au chocolates, entrecôte, frites, tomatoes.

Today's ride began with a road closure at the end of the road we were staying on, which required us to follow a deviation for a short distance. Almost immediately, we were stopped at a barrier blocking our bridge crossing before even getting out of Lorient. There was a queue of cars waiting at the barrier, and next to it were separate barriers, with queues for cyclists and pedestrians. We quickly realised that our choice of crossing, the Pont Gueydon, wouldn't be available to us as everyone was showing their 'Naval Group' security passes as they passed through. (Naval Group being a French naval defence company.) Fortunately, not so far upstream, we found a cycle-friendly crossing—a very nice new bridge, actually, the Pont de Indes. This was to be the first of 16 bridges that we crossed that day.

Just over 40 kilometres into today's ride and we have another decision to make. There's a strange-looking crooked finger of land pointing back in the direction of our travel up the coast, part of the Gavres-Quiberon, and there seems to be a cycle path travelling the length of it for about 7 or 8 kilometres. If we go up it, we then have to go back down it, or we don't go and consequently save 15 kilometres! It would have been criminal to miss it, but as there were no gendarmes in the vicinity, I think we were safe. It's a long run of sand dunes, some older with settled vegetation, some golden, and some possibly shifting. The point at which we join the 'finger', the dunes also stretch in the opposite direction, offering long, sweeping beaches and natural wildlife habitats.

We then arrived at Carnac, a place that I knew nothing about, but a Facebook follower, Michael Kennedy, advised that it's not a place to be missed!

There are thousands of standing stones in and around Carnac, and they are a bit mind-blowing, including a standing stone 6.50 metres tall. The standing stones were erected between 5,000 and 3,000 years B.C. However, we contrived to miss the stones; we saw possibly 3 stones—probably a rockery in someone's garden. We even followed Le Petit Train to see if it would lead us there; no luck, and it was going too slowly, so we overtook it and continued onwards, which seemed to provide some entertainment for those on board the train, some of whom clapped and cheered.

Carnac is stylish, and the resort has five beaches on the edge of pine trees with seaside residences. On the 2-kilometre Grande Plage, where we sat in glorious sunshine, the yacht club confirms the prestige of the place. At least we saw that, had a nice coffee, and sat enjoying our picnic, wondering who had stolen the stones and how!

So, it was a long ride to Vannes, passing by bays, beaches, pretty villages, and over the occasional bridge, of course. (As I mentioned, 16 in total, all of which have paths to cycle on, of different designs.)

As for Vannes, I hadn't realised it, but I had booked our accommodation near the old town, yet another nice romantic surprise with its cobbled alleyways, colourful mediaeval houses, restaurants, bars, and even a marina. Things to see for sure have been coming thick and fast. What an area to visit for a holiday!

Day 20, 16th June, distance 123.91 kilometres (2,190.95 kilometres), elevation gain 959m (20,901m).

Depart: Vannes Arrive: Guerande.

Weather: Light cloud, 19 degrees, no wind to concern us.

Food: Croissants, baguettes, fruit puree, yoghurt, cheeseburgers, frites, mackerel, rusks, gum sweets, and peanuts.

"Aren't we nearing the Pyrenees yet? This is going on forever. Is that a complaint, my preciousss? Nope."

Today we intend to cycle along the eastern shore of the Gulf of Morbihan. Another fascinating natural feature is a lot of small islands, with a microclimate warming its own inland sea. Somewhere I read that legend has it that there are as many islands in the gulf as there are days in the year; obviously there aren't—but there are a lot. This would make another great place to spend a week or two on holiday! However, we changed our route as it would take us down a peninsular to the Passage Saint-Armel, and whilst checking the route, I discovered that the foot passenger ferry there would not be running until 2 p.m.….we'd have been there by 10 a.m. I also had a fear that as the boatman rowed across, it would turn out to be the land of the dead and that we'd have to leave our souls behind. So instead, we passed over the 'Chenal de Saint-Leonarde' by the bridge just after Le Poulfanc. That's weird; I can't help feeling it should be Le Poulfanc'h, but it isn't. I did check.

Guerande was our destination today, a mediaeval town located in the department of Loire-Atlantique, Western France. Finally, we have escaped Brittany. (Though it has been great.) Which reminds me we have a rather big river to cross tomorrow. But for now, this peninsula overlooks the Pays Blanc—white land, named for its salt marshes. Consequently, the town's salt marshes make Guerande a renowned salt producer. Cycling through the salt marshes is fun, flat, and covers a surprisingly large area. Our planned route was to take us part way through the marshes, then out to Guerande, but Frodo, trailing just behind, wondered whether we could travel across them instead, as we were having a good time.

"I discovered it, I did, me and my preciousss. Way through the smelly, foggy salt marshes. Orcs don't come this way. Orcs don't know their secrets. They go around for days and days. Pedal quickly; soft and quick as ghosts we must be, my preciousss."

"So that's a yes, then?" checked Kate. Instead, we cycled across the marshes to a very large beach resort at Le Pouliguen Bay, cycling along the busy seafront beside a large sandy bay before doubling back to get to our destination, the mediaeval town of Guerande. The town is fortified, and the walls, in my opinion, are amongst the most complete and best preserved in France (Coincidentally it's also what the French say), but our stay is a few kilometres out of town.

Day 21, 17th June, distance 140.37 kilometres (2,331.32 kilometres), elevation gain 668m (21,569m).

Depart: Guerande. Arrive: Pornic.

Weather: Light cloud, light wind 21 degrees.

Food: Croissants, yoghurt, apple puree, bananas, baguettes, cereal bars, chews, chicken and veg, pancake rolls.

So, there is a lot of anticipation about today as we have the Loire blocking our route at Saint Nazaire. No problem; time for the Saint-Nazaire raid. There's a bridge there which could mean today's ride is about 60 kilometres; but it's a big one (and I've seen a few), this is possibly the scariest, most bum-clenching bridge to cross yet. Apparently, there is a free minibus service that takes cyclists, with their bikes, across, but not tandems. Or I understand there's a ferry about 80 kilometres away, which would mean today's ride is about 135 kilometres. That fails, and we're looking at about 180 kilometres to cross a bridge at Nantes, we could be getting to know the Loire rather well!

The Saint-Nazaire raid, though, recalls 'Operation Chariot' that took place on 28th March 1942. A British destroyer, HMS Campbeltown, had been modified to look like a German warship. At 1.30 am, it arrived in Saint-Nazaire harbour, rigged with delayed-action explosives, and rammed into the gates of a huge dock—the only dry dock large enough to house large German warships if they required repair. The plan worked and put the dock out of commission for the remainder of the war. It was costly for human life, with 169 people losing their lives and another 215 taken prisoner by the Germans.

This daring story puts our quandary into perspective, and perhaps tackling this bridge, when almost all advice says it is not safe to cross, is not worth risking our lives. We decided to set our sights for the free ferry crossing at Coueron, meaning a 135 kilometres ride today, but flat! The journey up stream was a bit industrial, for at least 20 kilometres or so, but the roads were quiet, and we were able to hold a good speed. The free ferry crossing was great; turned up and walked on, and the return leg back towards the bridge was more enjoyable, often alongside the river on bike paths and with café stops. It was good to have paid with our cowardice with those extra kilometres, but we did feel that it would have been an achievement to have gone over the bridge and perhaps wish we hadn't looked at the scare stories online. A slight regret then.

Day 22, 18th June, distance 113.17 kilometres (2,444.49 kilometres), elevation gain 282m (21,851m).

Depart: Pornic. Arrive: Les Sables-d'Olonne.

Weather: Thunderstorms, heavy rain, summer, and lightning, so we took shelter.

Food: Breton tarts, croissants, yoghurt, apricots, bananas, peanuts, sardines, bread sticks, rabbit terrine, tuna steak and vegetables, dark chocolate.

I woke up with a sense of regret—move on, John! Another day of anticipation—you wait for one, then two come together! Today the Ile de Noirmoutier is just off the coast, but, at low tide, the Gois Passage is revealed, a regularly flooded road when the tide is in that stretches more than 4 kilometres between Barbâtre and Beauvoir-sur-Mer and that can only be crossed at low tide. Bizarre to think that Le Tour has been across the Gois twice. The first was in 1999, when it caused chaos and a large crash, with riders injured or abandoning. It was used much more cautiously in 2011 as a 'neutralised start' with riders crossing in more of a procession until being waved off after clearing it. (The flag is waved to indicate the start of the race proper.)

If you want to take this route, first check the tide tables to see when you'll be able to cross. We didn't…need to. It had been raining all day, and we could see a storm rolling in over Noirmoutier. One thing that non-cyclists might not appreciate is how you become more attuned to the weather; changes in temperature when you are near a rain cloud; the wind picking up slightly as dark clouds get close; the direction the rain clouds are travelling; the warmth of the sun through thinner clouds; birds settling into trees as rain approaches and beginning to chirp as it passes and so on. (Forget cows, though, who knows what they are thinking? We saw one cow standing under a tree, taking shelter; the rest were sitting in an open field, looking totally miserable.) We could see the direction of travel of this storm and see the occasional flashes of lightning as it moved towards us, so we picked up speed, racing across its path rather than towards Noirmoutier and into it. This race lasted for the best part of an hour when the storm caught us just before we entered a town where we were able to shelter under a shop front until it passed.

We had avoided the electrical storm, but it continued to rain all day, so we just dug in and got on with it until we got hungry. At that point, we managed to find a bus shelter, so at least our baguette and sardines were dry, and I could take my helmet off and wring out my sodden cap. One of our daughters, Sarah, messaged us and made a comment about how lucky we were to be retired, on holiday, and eating lunch in a bus shelter. We were wet, a little cold, but not despondent. We sat chatting about how well we had done to pick up speed when we needed to and how we were able to manage the less than excellent weather. It's also surprising how nice baguette and sardines can be. We didn't sit around for too long, with another 45 kilometres to go. Helmets were back on, and we were back on our way. My sodden cycle cap felt uncomfortable when I put my helmet back on top, but sometimes it's best to just get on with what you have to do.

Les Sables-d'Olonne is the main fishing (and it seems to be yachting) port of the Vendée area. The area of 'Olonne' has been inhabited since before Roman times. The exact locations occupied evolved over time due to the changing coastline and the creation of a harbour in the 13th century. This has since expanded into the harbour of Les Sables-d'Olonne, protected from the ocean by a barrier of former sand dunes and navigated through a narrow channel. In the Middle Ages, Olonne exported goods such as wine and salt to ports in northern Europe; in the late 15th century, the settlement on the north of the harbour entrance—now the Les Chaumes quarter was fortified. Tourism boosted the town's fortunes at the start of the 19th century, thanks to its long expanses of sandy beaches. Even before the railway arrived in 1866, the town was a renowned bathing resort, but it then developed mainly as a seaside resort and subsequently as a yachting marina. The town is known internationally for the Vendée Globe, a challenge held there every four years. It is the world's toughest solo yacht race, where competitors race unaided and single-handed around the world in treacherous conditions.

Soaking wet, we were relieved to get into our hotel room, ready for a warm shower. Having removed my helmet and placed it on the side, something caught my eye—a snail had hitched a lift for the last 45 kilometres! The wet cap I put back on at lunchtime wasn't the cause of the discomfort after all; the snail was inside my helmet all the time. Luckily, it didn't have a crush on me.

Day 23, 19th June, distance 107. (2,551.95 kilometres), elevation gain 383m (22,234m).

Depart: Les Sables-d'Olonne. Arrive: La Rochelle.

Weather: rain until about 1.30, then dried up but a headwind for the last 50 kilometres tried to annoy me, but I ignored it.

Food: Fruit puree, bread, honey, bread, chocolate, peanuts, cereal bar, salad niçoise, pizza.

Les Sable-d'Olonne has some cycling history worth recalling. In the brutal 1919 Tour de France (TdF), stage 5 started here and finished in Bayonne, which was 482 kilometres—the longest ever stage of the TdF.

About 15 kilometres today, we passed Talmont-Saint-Hilaire. I read somewhere that Richard the Lionheart lived here, but I think he possibly stayed overnight in most places in the region. The history of the coast we have cycled beside for the last three weeks is often closely linked to Britain and is complicated and fascinating. Just in the case of Richard Coeur de Lion (8 September 1157–6 April 1199), he was King of England from 1189 until his death in 1199. He also ruled as Duke of Normandy, Aquitaine, and Gascony; Count of Poitiers, Anjou, Maine, and Nantes; and was overlord of Brittany at various times during the same period. He was the third of five sons of Henry II of England and Eleanor of Aquitaine and seemed unlikely to become king, but his two elder brothers died before the death of their father.

Another key road closure today pushed us further inland and added about 15 kilometres, but at least the weather was improving, giving us a lovely evening in La Rochelle. We have now cycled over 2,500 kilometres, so a 2-night stay allowed us a rest day! Yet again, we didn't physically feel we needed a rest, but in terms of the bigger picture, going all the way around France, maybe it has had an unknown positive impact. More importantly, we had time to discover the place.

La Rochelle! Back in 2014, we cycled from home to Bordeaux—direct. It only took us a leisurely 10 days on a cheap, heavy tandem. Here we are, having spent over 3 weeks cycling, and Bordeaux seems miles away. But it's time for a rest day, and having flirted with La Rochelle in the past, it was a nice opportunity to get to know her a bit more.

La Rochelle is a port town rich in culture and history. There's loads to see and do here, and much too much for us to fit in. Particularly when you're also trying to take it easy!

There's an undercover daily market in the quartier Saint Nicolas, an area with narrow cobbled streets and old buildings that was a joy to stroll through whilst there was a shower outside.

Guarding the entrance to the port are two 14th-century towers, the 'Tour Saint Nicolas' and the 'Tour de la Chaine'. There is also the oldest lighthouse on the Atlantic Coast, the Tour de la Lanterne. Once a navy prison, it has graffiti carved into the walls by prisoners. The time we had allowed us to visit the towers and get fabulous views over the city, port, and sea.

La Rochelle was one of the major trading ports and was the last sight thousands of emigrants saw before setting sail for the Americas. The Maritime

Museum is worth a visit, providing a historical perspective on the port as well as opportunities to board a variety of boats and see how those who work at sea live.

La Rochelle also has a connection to the history of the bicycle. The invention of the bicycle was almost like the race to reach the moon, with people competing to be the first to get there. There is still some confusion around who did what first with the first bicycle type machine, being the 'running machines', working similarly to young children's balance bikes of today but without steering! The first of these was in the late 1700s. But bicycles had been envisaged many years before, certainly in the late 1600s, by Jacques Ozanam, who could foresee advantages to an alternative to horses that ran under the power of the rider's own exertions. He went to the extent of commissioning a prototype by Dr Elie Richard. Richard, a doctor in La Rochelle, built, in about 1690, a carriage that could be steered. It was large and bulky, almost the size of a horse-drawn carriage, I think. An operator at the back of the vehicle propelled the machine by alternately pushing down on levers whilst the occupant sat at the front of the carriage. (Begins to sound more like a tandem.)

Looking forward to getting back on the bike, I advised Kate that tomorrow is even flatter. "It must be below sea level then!" said Kate.

Day 24, 21st June, distance 116.52 kilometres (2,668.47 kilometres), elevation gain 458m (22,692m).

Depart: La Rochelle. Arrive: Royan.

Weather: Sunny spells, 23 degrees, light breeze, and short cloudy spells.

Food: Pastries, baguettes, yoghurt, fruit puree, bananas, sweet chews, calamari, spaghetti bolognese, baguettes.

Our first place to head for today was Rochefort. What is it famous for? For one thing, not cheese. That would be Roquefort-sur-Soulzon, located in Iccitani, southern France. Rochefort is a naval town. We had visited Rochefort once before whilst on holiday. Probably in the 1980s. We visited the tourist office.

Kate, "I wonder if they have visits to the cheese factory?"

"I'm not sure that it's the same spelling." (Admittedly I didn't know.)

"We won't know if we don't ask." (True) Now, you must understand there were no search engines and smart phones then, but there are ways of asking that avoid that condescending question from bystanders that says, "How stupid are you?" (To be fair, I have more fear of getting things wrong than Kate; I'm usually more self-conscious.)

Kate, "Is it possible to visit the cheese factory?"

Reply, "Will that be the one about 500 kilometres from here?"

At least the answer suggests you're not alone in asking, but it is a bit like calling into The Black Horse in Stansted village, near Sevenoaks, and asking for directions to the airport!

"I think we should get a move on now, Kate."

"What's the Rochefort?"

We needed to find a crossing upstream from the busy road bridge over the Charente River. I had spotted what appeared to be a bridge, but it was unclear if it was okay for bikes. What a treat we were in for! It turned out to be 'Le Pont Transbordeur', a platform suspended from a trolley that ran on rails up above. It then travels back and forth from one side of the river to the other. (There wouldn't be a lot of point if it didn't.) As well as the cyclists and pedestrians that can currently cross, it used to allow cars, carts, and horses on board. The Rochefort Transporter Bridge is the last bridge of this type in France, and we were lucky as it has been renovated and only just reopened.

We then passed through the citadel of Brouage, an example of preserved military architecture that is designed in the shape of a star. Once a thriving port, it is now about 3 kilometres from the sea. Its importance was based around the salt industry. Brouage was the first important salt-trading town in France and the leading salt-trading port, employing thousands. However, the rise in the importance of its close neighbour, Rochefort (and its cheese exports), and the declining access to the citadel by ships as the sea receded led to its demise.

Our destination today was Royan, where there is a ferry crossing to Pointe de Grave and the amazing Piste Cyclables there, but that's our next day of riding. Royan is at the mouth of Gironde.

Allied bombings during the Second World War destroyed the town. Known then as the 'martyred city', it was declared a 'Laboratory of research on urbanism', and it is now a showcase of modernist architecture of the 1950s. Our stay was typical of that, with a distinctive variety of modernist buildings jutting out from amongst more traditional French houses. A very popular tourist destination with seafood restaurants, a beach, more seafood restaurants, and more beaches.

Day 25, 22nd June, distance 84.01 kilometres (2,752.48 kilometres), elevation gain 282m (22,974m).

Depart: Royan. Arrive: Lacanau-Ocean.

Weather: Sunny, light cloud, and a healthy sea breeze.

Food: Baguette, fruit loaf, fruit salad, yoghurt, pain au raisin, burrito, and side salad.

So, first, we needed to get the ferry across the Mersey, sorry, estuary. Having intended to leave at 9 a.m. for the 9.45 a.m. crossing, we accidentally left at 8.50 a.m. and somehow got the 9 a.m. ferry, which moved off as we walked along the car deck before we had parked the tandem.

We are at last south of the Gironde estuary, oh yes! Kate and I have spent many holidays in this area of the Gironde. Both before and then with our children. We loved the hot, sandy, surfing beaches, but also the pine forests that fringe the sand dunes behind the beaches. Then, a kilometre or two inlands, there are lakes that have sandy beaches, warm water, water sports, and wildlife. Amongst all of this, there are almost hidden 'Piste Cyclables' that provide a network of cycling options going to the warm lakes, bars, restaurants, and beaches. Pistes are often the only way to get to some secluded beaches and are such great fun. (Though we did get our first puncture of the trip. You've heard of porcupines; around here it's puncture pines.)

You can cycle for miles on them—today, all the way to our destination at Lacanau-Ocean. But we couldn't resist a ride down one of the old, broken-up routes for a few kilometres. These are the original pistes in this area. We came across them about 40 years ago! On sandy beaches, every few miles, there were bunkers (the German Atlantic Wall). To enable German messengers on motorbikes to travel quickly between them, they laid concrete blocks through the pine forests and over sand dunes. Subsequently, they have been great for cycling to secluded beaches and seaside resorts. Ultimately, they have deteriorated, but many have been replaced with amazing tarmac surfaces; the originals remain a great adventure—perhaps for investigating on mountain bikes! If the path wasn't bad enough, we eventually came to a warning sign, 'Piste deterioree, interdite au cycliste', which I took as a hint to take the turning up to the upgraded track.

So, another rest day already. What comes to mind? Surfing, skateboarding, dining out, tourist markets, fireworks, and mile after mile of beaches, BBQ's, beer, campsites, and dunes. A holiday paradise. We had a great rest and a meal in one of our favourite restaurants, La Cabane, all totally necessary!

Day 26, 24th June, distance 111.30 kilometres (2,863.78 kilometres), elevation gain 409 m (23,383m) Depart: Lacanau-Ocean. Arrive: Arcachon.

Weather: sunny, 29 degrees; gentle sea breeze and pine shade kept it pleasant, just as we expected here.

Food: Breakfast biscuit, bread, honey, fruit puree, banana, baguette, tuna, last of the chewy sweets, goat cheese salad, chicken, spinach lasagne, grilled tomato.

Back onto the glorious Piste Cyclable, passing quickly past Lacanau Lake (not within sight) and then through a naturist holiday camp. I have to say, I just could not do it. I take off my hat to them, but that's about all, chapeau! But riding without a chamois, nope. Not only that, but I have one of those saddles that have a gap running down the middle…no, I don't even want to think about it. Too late.

Joyful cycling, no cars just fun all the way to the Bay of Arcachon and Cap Ferret, with a gentle breeze and pine tree shade keeping us cool. It's about 45 kilometres from Cap Ferret, with swimming and surfing beaches and views over to the spectacular Dune of Pilat on the opposite side of Arcachon Bay. The Phare du Cap Ferret is a prominent landmark here. Slightly expensive bars and restaurants are hidden away, as are fishermen's cottages and quaint ports used for oyster farming.

The Bay of Arcachon is famous for its oysters and resorts, such as Arcachon and Le Cap Ferret. This tidal bay has a mild climate and plenty of sunshine for much of the year. Quaint authentic oyster villages are dotted around the bay, and plenty of cheaper seafood restaurants can be found. It's a popular place for walking and bird watching, as well as tourist attractions such as the Aqua Park, a theme park, and the Zoo.

Our destination today turned out to be 1 kilometre from a Decathlon, don't mention it to Kate.

Kate, "Do you know we just cycled past a Decathlon without stopping?"

"Er, yes, I thought we'd get a shower, lock the bike up safely, and stroll up for a proper look." (I think I got away with that.)

Luckily, of course, we have no room to carry purchases, so this will be a cheap night out. Wrong, we came back with a new waterproof bag for the back of the bike (eyes look in top of head time)—well, at least we can just put the old bag in it. No, that is not what I meant!

Day 27, 25th June, distance 140.73 kilometres (3,004.51 kilometres), elevation gain 752m (24,135m).

Depart: Arcachon. Arrive: Vieux-Boucau-Les-Bains.

Weather: Same as yesterday, this is so nice.

Food: Fruit cocktail, apple puree, pain au raisin, cereal, baguette, biscotti, breakfast bar, Kit Kat, lamb chops, frites, lettuce, pate, bread.

At the entrance to the Bay of Arcachon, the Dune du Pilat is the highest sand dune in Europe, about 100 metres high and 3 kilometres long. If you struggled to picture this, so did I. It's impressively humongous—does that help? I was amazed and grateful that we had been able to cycle beside it. But it is just a pile of sand.

Landes has a reputation for being boring, so let me do that justice. It does give us a flat ride. The cycle route from Arcachon to Vieux-Boucau-Les-Bains is a mundane journey. The route begins in Arcachon and follows a series of unremarkable roads and cycle paths that wind through various uninteresting towns and villages, including La Teste-de-Buch (near the start), Gujan-Mestras (a bit further along), and Biscarrosse Plage. (Not much further along.)

The landscape along the way is mostly flat and featureless, with few noteworthy sights or landmarks to break up the monotony. We occasionally caught a glimpse of some nondescript forests or fields, but these offered little in the way of visual interest or stimulation.

As the journey progressed, the cycle path occasionally merged with busy roads, forcing us to navigate through unappealing industrial areas and uninspiring suburban sprawl. The cycle path is also poorly maintained in places, with cracked pavements and occasional patches of gravel that can make for an uncomfortable and precarious ride.

After several hours of tedious pedalling, we eventually reached our destination: Vieux-Boucau-Les-Bains, a forgettable coastal town with little to distinguish it from countless other seaside resorts in the region. Overall, the cycle from Arcachon to Vieux-Boucau-Les-Bains is a bland and unremarkable experience that is likely to uninspire or gently sedate even the most avid cycling enthusiasts.

Was that fair? No, not really. Our route took us to some pleasant coastal resorts, lakeside beaches, and fast and fun cycling paths. We did have a couple of issues on the journey, however. The first was shortly after the Dune du Pilat, when we should have been on a coastal route, but our turning was blocked for 'Traveaux Forestiere'. That wasn't so bad, though, with our route reappearing just a few kilometres down the road in the form of pleasant forest pistes. The bigger issue came after a coffee stop at Biscarrosse Plage. We knew that we had to travel inland to Biscarrosse and loop around the Etang de Biscarrosse due to a military zone blocking what would otherwise be a short cut. We did that but having cycled 5 kilometres down a road to rejoin our route, we found the road blocked by a military barrier and two gates. The gate on the right came from the direction we knew was out of bounds, but the gate on the left we had hoped was a forest track to continue our journey. After a few minutes of indecision, I decided to lift the receiver off the wall-mounted phone and see if I could negotiate, aware that we were probably being watched by the multiple CCTV cameras glaring at us:

"Bonjour."

"Bonjour, parlez-vous Anglais?" The problem when I say this is that they think I at least speak a little French.

"Non, que voulez-vous?"

"Pardon, je suis Anglais, je ne parle pas Français," now they think I speak a lot of French.

"Bonjour."

"Bonjour" (back down to my level.)

The conversation that I did not comprehend continued for a few more responses, and then I could hear what I assumed was a handover taking place until a new voice came onto the call, "Bonjour."

"Bonjour, Parlez-vous Anglais?"

"Pas très bien, juste un peu…just a little."

"We are cycling to Boucau, but the gate is closed."

"Vous devez revenir en arrière comme vous êtes venu…You need to go back."

"We are on a bicycle, and have just cycled 5 kilometres from Biscarrosse."

"You can't go; you have to go back."

"We would have to cycle 5 kilometres back and then find a detour to Boucau? That is a long way on a bicycle."

"You can't go; you have to go back."

"Okay, merci beaucoup!" I say, with a sigh of defeat. I know this is our problem, not theirs, but in this situation, a little person on the phone never thinks that they'll consult with someone and check that a small rule can't be broken; some advice about the best route, some endeavour that might demonstrate empathy with the situation, perhaps a check that you have enough fluids for the journey—just some degree of humanity. We quickly had something to eat, did a wee in the bushes in full sight of the CCTV cameras (possibly), and then cycled back to Biscarrosse to discover that we now had about a 20 kilometres detour via Parentis on less than pleasant roads. Generally, it was a bit boring for large sections of the ride, though a slight detour to Mimizan allowed us to enjoy a delightful section beside the Lac de Biscarrosse et de Parentis.

Vieux Boucau, meaning 'old mouth', was once Port d'Albret. It would be the first port on the Landes coast if the river L'Adour had not been diverted in 1578 through Bayonne. Lac Marin was created in 1966. Before its creation, the town was faced with regular silting of the old river mouth. Many projects followed, including the construction of dykes. In the spring of 1975, a Dutch dredge arrived by sea to dig the canal and the marine lake that are now in place, and since then, a whole tourist complex has been built around the marine lake. It's a clever feat of engineering, and we had a nice meal by the harbour before strolling around it.

<u>Day 28</u>, 26th June, distance 109.50 kilometres (3114.01 kilometres), elevation gain 1,145m (25,280m).

Depart: Vieux-Boucau-Les-Bains. Arrive: Sare.

Weather: Overcast but a pleasant 22 degrees, could be nice for climbing mountains; but could be wet.

Food: Croissants, baguettes, marmalade, apricots, strawberries, yoghurt, mackerel, sultanas, peanuts, cereal biscuits, charcuterie, and beef stew.

Leaving on fast, flat, and pleasant roads, around the harbour at Capbreton, then onto Bayonne and over the rerouted river L'Adour, it is not long before we reach Biarritz, which is located 35 kilometres from the border with Spain. (Pyrenees here we come.) It is known for its surfing, beaches, casinos, and restaurants. (It feels like I have cut and pasted that sentence several times on this coast!) We have enjoyed some stays in Biarritz over the years—the surf is usually really good—and it would have been nice to have a coffee there, but it can be very busy, and we passed through almost before realising it. That turned out to be the best, as it allowed us to discover Saint Jean de Luz, which is located midway between Biarritz and the border with Spain. We haven't hit the main holiday season yet, and it was a little busy, but not like Biarritz. The ancient part of town has buildings that date back to the 17th century, a time when the main economic activity changed from fishing to piracy, a base for Basque corsairs. With the blessing of the king of France, these corsairs would find and chase down France's enemies at sea, doing what pirates do. They were feared by both the

British and the Spanish, who were the main victims of the pirates who brought back their plunder to Saint Jean de Luz.

We turned left at Hendaye; France and Spain at this point have a natural border, the river Bidasoa. Coming down from white water rapids in the mountains and formed from multiple streams and small rivers, it empties into the Bay of Biscay here. At this point, we almost crossed a bridge, the Pont International; if we had, we'd have entered Spain, and at that point, in the middle of the river, just downstream, there's a small island. Right, so France on this side and Spain, on the other, which one owns the island? The puzzle gets more complicated; if you look on Google Maps you can see the line showing the border that runs down the centre of the river, but when it gets to the island, 'Pheasant Island', it splits, encircling it—so it belongs to no one then? No, this takes some explaining and has historical importance. On the island is a monument that commemorates the Treaty of the Pyrenees, negotiated here in 1659. The name of the island is a misnomer, as there are no pheasants here and very rarely any peasants. Back in Roman times, the island had a very appropriate name, 'Pausoa' meaning passage or step. It is believed that the French translated this to 'Paysans', meaning peasant, subsequently amending it to 'Faisans' (Pheasant). That explains the name—the easy bit!

At the end of what was called the Thirty Years War (1618–1648), following a ceasefire between France and Spain, the island was chosen as a neutral spot to agree on new borders, ultimately resulting in the Treaty of the Pyrenees a decade later. To honour this, a royal wedding took place on the island, and it became so symbolic, a metaphor for peace, that it was agreed that Spain and France would have joint custody. (No oil under there then.) It would be Spanish from February to July and French from August to January. I have a feeling you may be doubting me, but it's true. So given just over a month's time, we could have gone onto the island whilst remaining in France if we had a rowing boat.

We have turned east, and gently begun to climb. Nothing too bad, just enough to begin to warm up the legs and warn the different muscle groups that their turn is coming! Even, to our surprise, ticking off a climb, the Col de Saint Ignace. But Kate was enjoying a new experience all together. Taken she enough food not had—she bonked and was struggling to get her worms out correctly. The buzzards began to circle overhead. (Honestly, they did.)

Our destination was Sare. I viewed it as a place in the foothills of the Pyrenees and little more than that, but the place I had booked to stay, just out of town, was very quaint, and we soon discovered that the Basque town itself was a pleasant place to visit. Kate, though, by now was very quiet and confessed that she really didn't feel well. Finding that we then had to go at least 1 kilometre uphill to walk into town did not help. We found a restaurant and reserved a table, allowing us enough time to look around. But first, off to a shop for peanuts, sultanas, cereal bars, and fig rolls, all eaten by Kate whilst waiting for the restaurant to open! She almost recovered well enough to feign interest in the things there were to see: a Basque church (17th century Church of Saint Martin); a graveyard plaque honouring a hero of the Second World War; a Pelote pitch for a Basque sport that sounds a bit like fives. But then, in fact, we had a really good meal, and that was all that mattered (to Kate).

Day 29, 27th June, distance 63.09 kilometres (3,177.1 kilometres), elevation gain 1,408 m (26,688m).

Depart: Sare. Arrive: Arneguy.

Weather: overcast but mild (20 degrees); get the feeling we are going to get wet any day now.

Food: Basque tarts, baguettes, yoghurts, bananas, omelettes, bread, fig rolls, pasta bolognaises, apricot yoghurt, pancakes, green salad.

As we left Sare, we got stuck behind a herd of sheep being shepherded down the road by a farmer in a white van—not something you see every day. We could see a crossroads ahead, and next to the road straight on was an open gate into a farmyard, evidently where the sheep were headed. But then, in a garden on the left, a gardener started up his petrol strimmer, and we had mayhem. The sheep bolted along the road towards the main road. The farmer yelled at the gardener, who immediately shut the strimmer off. The farmer then started shouting "Stop, stop!" as the sheep ran across the main road, causing vehicles in both directions to screech to a stop, in turn startling the sheep further. They were now headed down the road straight ahead rather than through the gate…somehow the repeated shouts of 'stop' actually brought them to a halt, and the farmer, now out of his vehicle, was able to coax them 'round and back through the farm gate. This could be one of those days!

The mountains have arrived, so a start hilly enough to reintroduce the legs to climbing…up to Gastigarlepoa, 4.5 kilometres at an average of 5.8%, that wasn't so bad. It is what you don't know that catches you out. We'd had a few ramps up on the climbs, just short 15% sections, but what was waiting for us after the climb were longer sections of around 20%. It was a relief to reach Saint-Jean-

Pied-de-Port, where we stopped to eat in a bar/restaurant 10 kilometres from the finish and enjoyed an alcohol-free beer and a cheese omelette. (We knew there was no restaurant nearby tonight.)

In Arneguy, we popped into a Spanish supermarket to buy an evening meal, fluids, and tomorrow's breakfast. Unfortunately, this was difficult to fit into our haversack and was rather heavy and pokey in the back. We carry a packable haversack for these occasions.

"I'll carry it when we need to shop," said Kate when we were planning the tour. It's really heavy and pokey in the back now that we are on tour.

Our overnight stop is about 4 kilometres southwest of Arneguy, on the border with Spain. The village of Arneguy is in an agricultural area and is a stopping point on the road between Saint-Jean-Pied-de-Port and Pamplona, Spain, as it lies on the border. But those 4 kilometres turned out to be the slowest of the day, with steep, winding roads going up and up, ultimately getting close to 20%. And it hadn't happened before (hasn't happened since), but both our Garmin's were playing up, and mine read 2.4 kilometres to go when Kate's read 3 miles. The haversack's contents were by now protruding painfully into my back, and the shoulder straps felt more like chain cilice strapped to each shoulder. And having reached the 2.4 kilometres, my Garmin now said there were no metres left to go, but the route seemed to continue for another 1 kilometre whilst Kate's was still at about 1.5 miles to go. That was enough. We stopped to try to work out what was happening before noticing, about 50 metres ahead the converted barn on the next bend. What a relief!

That evening we ate our shop bought meal, shared the 'pokey in the back' bottle of wine, changed the rear disc brake pad, checked our Garmin's, which were now okay and went to bed wondering, apprehensively, what the rest of this climb that we had just started was going to be like in the morning. (By that, I don't mean miraculously level out.)

Day 30, 28th June, distance 81.29 kilometres (3,258.39 kilometres), elevation gain 2,534m (29,222m).

Depart: Arneguy. Arrive: Tardets-Sorholus.

Weather: Overcast, some sunny spells above the clouds.

Food: Pancakes, yoghurt, bread, honey, banana, baguette, chocolate biscuit, cereal bar, charcuterie plate, grilled chicken, new potatoes, sheep cheese with jam.

I woke up, threw open the shutters, and could not believe what I was seeing. Somehow, the terrain had miraculously levelled out overnight.

For the next 10 days, shorter distances, lots of climbing, and real snail mode. We started to climb immediately today, for about 10 kilometres, ascending about 1,000 metres, then got two or three kilometres to recover, then dropped all that height to start all over again. It starts.

But this really doesn't do the thing justice. This was one of our hardest days of cycling ever. Both ascents had regular, long sections that were between 14-20%. We dug in after 500m averaging 24.5% near the start. On Facebook that evening, I posted a photo, commenting that we had stopped taking breathers after five hundred metres at an average of twenty-four and a half percent. Sarah Wooller, a Facebook follower, commented, "Oh, that just sounds like hell," and when I replied that I wasn't sure because I'd never been there, she said, "…you don't need to now. You already bought the T-shirt."

I developed an aching right arm from the constant need to balance the bike at about walking pace. Legs could push no harder without risk of muscles twanging; it was a real strain. When we hit a section like this, we keep going. Firstly, if we stop, it will be almost impossible to start again. Secondly, stopping isn't that easy on a steep incline. The tandem is under immense strain on a section like this; it begins to creak, and worrying clicks can be heard. It is a bit stressful; you worry the chain may snap, the gears may jam, and an inconsiderate driver may get in our way. Later (at the end of the day), you do get an amazing sense of achievement—but that's later. We reach a point where the road flattens, but we sense that it's temporary, so we stop to consider a change from our usual tactic, which is just to relentlessly grind on. We tend not to consider that we may not be able to do this type of challenge, but perhaps we need to consider how best to manage it. We have the same approach in mind as each other (always useful), which is to tackle a bit at a time, have regular stops for snacks and fluids, and admire the views. It's slow, almost laborious, but it's successful. We didn't know it, but it turned out to be the toughest day of the tour and put all the other climbs in context, but the views were incredible.

A couple of things to say about Torre de Urkulu (close to the top of our first ascent) 1. It's in Spain. 2. It's not in France. However, getting so close to the borders of other countries does mean we can, on occasion, see some interesting landmarks. The Urkulu Trophy Tower is a Roman commemorative tower located at the top of Mount Urkulu (1,419 metres above sea level), a confirmation that we've already started to do some significant climbing. The tower is in the shape of an upturned cone with the top levelled off. It is thought to have been constructed in 28 BC by the proconsul Marco Valerio Mesala Corvino to commemorate his victory in the Pyrenees over the Tarbelos. You will appreciate at this point that I have no idea what I am talking about. In 1976, a French archaeologist Jean-Luc Tobie identified it as a Roman trophy tower, erected in the 1st century BC to commemorate the conquest of Aquitaine. The construction was used to mark the southern limit of the newly conquered territories. (That bit, I understand.)

There weren't too many scary vertigo, teetering on the edge, moments today, but they did exist. Sarah Wooller, commented that she had never suffered vertigo until she met French hills, and I explained that I have to focus on the road to cope. Sarah replied, "…not when you get vertigo, then you have to get off quick and sit down because you can't find horizontal," but she wasn't fooling me; "You are getting confused with alcohol."

Cycling over the high, remote mountains, you expect to be in the wilderness, and today really felt isolated, something that Kate was ill at ease with. (She had, after all, had a near-death experience where the quick response of emergency medical personnel saved her life.) But you occasionally come across homesteads, holiday homes, villages, and evidence from the past. Today we passed through valleys that, like many mountainous Pyrenean valleys, were a centre of mines and metallurgy. Between the mid-18th and 19th century several forges operated in the area. The most significant was the Udoipeia forge (pronounced fawj), employing about 150 people. The iron ore was transported by mule or on the back of a man. The nearby stream provided the energy for the mechanical machinery that struck the iron.

Smelting and metalworking required large quantities of charcoal, and this was produced in local forests by charcoal burners. The forge consumed the equivalent of 7 hectares of forest every year! Metal fabrication methods are, at first, very primitive. It took hours to heat the ore with bellows and to hammer the cast iron in order to obtain, well, just a small amount of iron, which was actually of very poor quality. Oh, well, so much for that. Improvements were made gradually, and by 1790, a much more powerful wind tunnel system operated. Around 1836-1837, a blast furnace 10 metres high was built. But despite the technical improvements and the skilled workforce, the forge of Udoipeia produced as much profit as a pro-Brexit fundraising stall in Strasbourg. There were multiple barriers: a mediocre quality ore extracted some distance from the workshop, in the mountains, in veins that were quickly exhausted; the Pyrenean Mountain climate that was not always friendly—in 1800, a violent storm destroyed the site; the metal produced, in small quantities, had to be transported to Tardets, 20 kilometres away on the back of a mule! You'd think a cargo bike would have been better! Ultimately, the location of the forge meant it was doomed.

So, 20 kilometres later, our destination was indeed Tardets-Sorholus—they travelled this far with their produce on the back of a mule; it's unimaginable. It was not even flat, but a lovely, smooth road, though.

Booking our stops when going across mountain ranges is firstly about convenience, but it's always a nice surprise when it's not just a hut on top of an imminent landslide. Over the centuries, the dwellings here in Tardets may well have been altered, as have the roadways, though cobbles are still present. As you walk, you see coloured facades, carved wooden doors of ancient houses, and even the alleyways are delightful. The town has some shops, a small campsite, and a couple of restaurants. It's been a tough day; there's a sense of relief but also a sense of achievement to have got through it, but as usual, a shower and a nice meal, and all is great again.

"Is every day going to be as tough as that? With the gear on, some of that was a real challenge." I reassured Kate that it wasn't going to be like that. We know most of the other climbs, and they may be long and high, but they are nowhere as steep. The fact that we were able to do what we did today was, in fact, reassuring for the rest of the trip.

Day 31, 29th June, distance 56.43 kilometres (3,314.82 kilometres), elevation gain 1,618m (30,840m).

Depart: Tardets-Sorholus. Arrive: Osse-en-Aspe.

Weather: Drizzle to be generous, low cloud, damp, not warm. To be less than generous and bloody miserable.

Food: Pain au chocolate, yoghurt, baguette, croissant, peanuts, raisins, Spanish tortilla, lettuce, soup, garlic bread, fruit purées, banana, chocolate biscuits.

So, how do the legs feel after such a tough day? Not a twinge. My arm? Fine. I ask Kate how she is, "No aches or pains. Wondering at the time; can we get up that climb? But you do; it feels great, and by the following morning, it's like a brand-new start. Is it a bit flatter today?"

The answer is yes. Yesterday was the only day I had no real insight into the Pyrenees or the Alps. I said to Kate, "After what we achieved yesterday, we are good to go; nothing compares."

La Pierre de San Martin is a high mountain pass at an elevation of 1,760 metres located right on the border with, and can be climbed from, the Spanish side. The road we took did not go all the way there but peaked at the Col du Soudet. The Col du Soudet was a climb into the Tour de France, memorably continuing up to La Pierre de San Martin in 2015, when Chris Froome beat his rivals by over a minute to take a grip on the general classification. Our route took us up the opposite side (west) from Licq-Atharay; the climb from this side is about 21.5 kilometres long. The average gradient is probably about 5–7% for the last 10 kilometres, but there seemed to be a much steeper section in the middle somewhere. What do you expect? 5% is just the average. In any case, doesn't it all sound so much easier than yesterday.

It was a short ride today, though, so no rush. I remember watching that stage of the tour and seeing the peloton flying up the smooth road through a beautiful valley with lush green meadows. I remember thinking it was quite an easy climb then. But then the leaders began to run out of energy; Contador, Van Garderan, and Nibali were dropped, leaving Richie Porte to drag teammate Chris Froome for as long as he could before 'boom'! Off went Froome with about 6 kilometres to go, with his ludicrous cadence, elbows out, and watching a documentary about edible snails on his bike computer, leaving Quintana standing. Porte was able to track Quintana, slowly reeling him in and then doing himself and Froome a favour by sprinting past with about 300 metres to go.

The Bosley snail went up to Col du Soudet, leaving a slimy, silvery blue Garmin trail behind us and little else—a pattern for a few days to come—what a way to kick off the Tour de France climbs of the Pyrenees. On the way up the climb, road signs appeared every kilometre to give cyclists an update on their progress. Signs like this are typical on the climbs of the grand tours (and others) they remind you of the climb's altitude and what climb you're on for when you start to get confused. They also say how many kilometres there are left to go and the average gradient for the next kilometre. I stress that on average, if you plummet downhill just after the sign, you're in for a shocking last 400m of that kilometre.

On the way to Osse-en-Aspe, there were a few kilometres of gentle climbing to get over the Col de Bouesou, then downhill all the way. That little climb was welcome; we had descended into drizzle with about 30 metres of visibility, and we were starting to get cold. The short climb warmed us up again before the beautiful, wooded descent, not too steep, that would have been tranquil and beautiful in the sun. You might imagine we'd be thinking, oh no, another climb, but I was literally looking at the profile and letting Kate know that there was a climb coming that would warm us up again. It wasn't the last time we wanted to climb because we were cold.

Osse-en-Aspe looked like a nice place, but when the weather is damp and cold, it's difficult to really look around. Added to that, when there is no shop or restaurant open, you have other priorities to deal with. We had arrived early, but a quick message to the host of the Chambre d'hôte was answered immediately with, "Your room is all ready for you; see you soon." As we cycled up the road, I spotted the shape of a heart on the hillside. It was very cleverly crafted, with the top 'm' shape created from the edge of a tree line and the bottom 'v' from the point at which the slope of a hillside passes in front of another hill.

As soon as we arrived (10 minutes later), we were offered the use of the washing machine and dryer, which was very generous. Our host advised that she did not do evening meals but could book a table for us at a nearby restaurant whilst we got showered (rude!). She had to then inform us that the restaurant was closed, but she could throw something together for us for 10 euros each. What a relief! We were delighted. She threw together a basic, though delicious, 3-course meal with wine. People can be amazing.

Day 32, 30th June, distance 85.81 kilometres (3,400.63 kilometres), elevation gain 2,299m (33,139m).

Depart: Osse-en-Aspe. Arrive: Arcizans-Dessus.

Weather: rain for the first hour, then gradually cleared but mainly overcast (well, it's not July yet.)

Food: Yoghurt, pancakes, baguettes, cold meats, chocolate biscuits, peanuts, fruit salad, couscous, pasta salad, crisps. Three Cols to conquer today, though it's a bit of a 'buy two, get another one free', none the less a little daunting.

First, up the Col de Marie-Blanque. In fact, first we had to get there in torrential rain for about 10 kilometres, and what is it about slugs around here? If you know of Jabba the Hut, you are well on the way to picturing them. I decided that if we went over one, it would probably take us down. A Facebook follower, Tom Crispin, without prompting, commented, "I remember the Pyrenean rain well. The thing is, just five miles to the south, over the border in Spain, it is probably as dry as a bone. We camped when we traversed the Pyrenees. Climbing into a small bikepacking tent pitched in a swamp is a character-building exercise. And then there were the giant slugs…Snails around France do try (riding over one) at least once. They make a sound somewhere between a satisfying squelch and a pop." I wasn't taking the risk.

The climb from Escot to begin with is only 2%, or possibly 3%. Of course, if the average is supposed to be about 7%, it's easy to think this won't be so bad after all. Then you remember that if too much is easy over the course of 9 kilometres, especially if there's a bit of downhill, then the rest is even harder. But no, the incline seems to rise very gradually, with very few bends on the way, and it seems an age before we get to gradients that are supposed to be the average, at least 5 or 6 kilometres.

Now, I always get this bit wrong. I have information about our route; do I share it with Kate? Does she like to know what I think may be coming up, or was it the last time I said 'only 3 kilometres to go' that she went all 'rabid Rottweiler' on me because she thought it was just 1 kilometre. I'm not sure, but I'll play safe and keep quiet.

At about 3.5 kilometres to go, the road went up with a kick. "Ah, this is it!"

"What do you mean, this is it?"

"Shit!" (tutted to myself) "Err, the life!"

"The life? What do you mean?"

"This is the life."

"Oh."

We had arrived at a gate used for closing the pass in inclement, wintry weather, and suddenly we were going rather slowly.

"Why are we going so slowly?" Kate asked.

"It's easier to take in the views." I said.

The gradient is fluctuating between ten and twelve percent, and at one point, my Garmin was saying 14%. Those last few kilometres were a grind, but they were at least steady—no big kick-ups; we just had to dig in and keep to a rhythm. A cyclist passed us during this section (very slowly, of course!) and wished us well. When we reached the summit, he, Bernard, was still there, so we briefly shared our stories and goals. He was traversing the Pyrenees, though his friend 'Jeff' was less in love with the climbs and had taken a different route today. We were destined to meet them a few times over the next few days, usually on the way up or at the top of the mountains. We took a selfie with Bernard, with the Col sign in the background.

To be honest, that was just the warm-up. Now, a monster climb, the Col d'Aubisque, and a legend of the Tour de France. The one that was recommended to me by a Facebook follower, 'Bed Breakfast Bikes Pyrenees', "The Aubisque is stunning. We did it on our tandem a few years ago. Of the ones we've done over the Haute Pyrenees, the Aubisque is our favourite!" A 17-kilometre climb averaging 7% and uphill non-stop all the way. Riding out of the town of Laruns, and it's a gentle start…oh no, here we go again. Right, just forget it, relax, and enjoy.

It may seem odd, but I often worry that I'll miss the top of a climb, but not here. Three enormous bikes—yellow, green, and, of course, white with red polka-dots, representing the TdF jerseys—dominate. Actually, that's not true; the surrounding mountains still win the domination stakes. Yellow to represent the yellow jersey (the Maillot Jaune) which is awarded to and worn by the overall race leader. Green, the colour of the jersey representing the rider who is leading the points classification from points gained from the position they finish on each stage and intermediate sprints on the route, is often called the sprinters jersey. The polka dot jersey, awarded to the leader of the best climber classification, points are awarded for getting to the top of climbs ahead of other riders.

There's a memorial at the top to Andre Bach (1888–1945) that reads (in French):

Officer of the Legion of Honour, President of the Cyclo Club Béarnais (CCB).

Death during deportation. This is to perpetuate his memory in this place he loved so much. His friends, the CCB cycle tourists. Although his left arm was amputated in Verdun in 1916, André BACH was a passionate cyclist, a lover of the Pyrenean passes, and especially of his favourite, the Aubisque. He rode it several times, from 1937, with his friends from the Cyclo Club Bearnais, of which he was the president.

He loved to write and became a journalist and then editor of the Independent in Pau. He wrote several great articles about sport, especially about cycle tourism.

A courageous man, 'Father Bach' joined the Resistance in 1940 and travelled thousands of kilometres on his bike for it, in Bearn but also as far as the Swiss border. Arrested on August 8, 1943, and deported to Buchenwald, he died exhausted on May 10, 1945.

Every year since 1947, the Bearnais cycling club meets around this memorial, which they have erected in his honour. But it is also an honour to all the members of the club and the other cyclists who have ridden up the pass 'using muscle strength and will/determination'.

"I know few pleasures equivalent to those of climbing a pass, of finding the way through the mountain, which defends itself using the steepness, of fighting against this gradient, of resisting all temptations—that of the water bottle handed over by a friend and the call of the spring water which trickles down—of refusing to get off the bike and walk in the mountains, to give 'the honours of the foot' to the mountain, and, finally, when it's possible—because it's not always possible—of overcoming and reaching the top with all the satisfaction of duty accomplished and the landscape won by the muscle strength and will/determination." Andre Bach (Excerpt from 'Queen of Steel, Queen of the Collars' Cycle magazine—1941) (Thanks to Alison Millar, a French language teacher, for helping with the translation.)

The Col de Soulor gets a passing mention, but in this direction, you conquer it by just going gently up and over its peak on your way down (I made that sound slightly easier than reality.)

It seemed unlikely that we would be able to find a restaurant near our destination today, and having failed to find cafés or restaurants on the descent, we ended up feasting on food from a shop, only to discover that our stay had what looked like a gourmet restaurant. The type of error you really regret!

Oh, there may be trouble ahead. Kate's decided to take the route with the climbing profiles on her Garmin to give her some more things to follow as we snail along. (And more things to question, like: Why have you diverted from the planned route? Why didn't we stop at that café when it looked likely to be the last one today? Why are we staying in this youth hostel when there's a Hilton just 500 metres up the road?)

<u>Day 33</u>, 1st July, distance 61.68 kilometres (3,462.31 kilometres), elevation gain 1,741m (34,880m).

Depart: Arcizans-Dessus. Arrive: Campan.

Weather: dry, overcast, about 16 degrees. Colder at the top! (It's tough at the top.)

Food: Cake, pain au chocolate, baguette, yoghurt, cereal bar, pancake, ½ pizza, apple crumble tart, ½ portion of fish, chips, and mushy peas.

I described this as one of our 'recovery' days, with only 60 kilometres and less than 2,000m of climbing. Our Facebook follower, Tom commented, "Col du Tourmalet a 'recovery ride'. I just love your style. I came closer to death riding up there than anything else I have ever done. I was so concerned for your worldly well-being when you didn't post on Facebook yesterday evening that I had to check your Strava page for confirmation that you'd made the climb alive." If you are unfamiliar with Strava, in brief, it analyses your exercise. (Walking, running, cycling, etc.) It enables you to keep track of your performance and activity whilst sharing this with others who may not use the same recording system as you. (e.g., Garmin, Wahoo, or Polar) It also records the route you have taken and allows you to find routes you have not taken before based on the data of other users.

I couldn't believe that after conquering the climbs yesterday, we were facing the Tourmalet today. We had wanted to cycle it a few years ago from the opposite direction, but poor weather rerouted us (not true, I rerouted us due to poor weather conditions.) In cycling, there are several French climbs that are considered legendary. Mont Ventoux and the Tourmalet are the two most revered. But before that lies the town of Luz-Saint-Sauveur, or just 'Luz'. Famous for what, its bridge commissioned by Napoleon III? Its fortified church, 'The Templars'? No, most likely that Luz is the start of the western approach to the Tourmalet.

19 kilometres long and, guess what? An average gradient of 7%. In fact, you reach Barèges possibly 6 or 7 kilometres in before the gradient goes up and zooms straight past 7%. We rode a few kilometres with Greet, a Belgian cyclist. The chat on the way up had helped make the climb go by more easily, but we slowed to drink and eat during the steeper section and waved her to go on. It was nice to see her again briefly to congratulate each other at the top of the climb.

The steep final kilometre at last gets us to the summit. I couldn't miss it; it's marked by a giant statue of Octave Lapize, the first rider to conquer the Tourmalet, whilst labelling the race organisers 'murderers' for including such a mountain in a bike race. Now downhill, and that famous story enters my head about Monsieur Eugene Christophe. What happens if you're leading the Tour de France and your front forks snap? Easy, you check you are still alive, your team car arrives with a replacement bike, and you speed on, hopefully maintaining your lead. You don't do it in 1913.

I pictured myself as Christophe, in tears, looking down in disbelief at my broken forks and knowing that my rivals would be passing me in just a few minutes. A motorcycle passes. "What can I do?" I'm in tears, all the hard work for nothing, my dream stolen from me.

"Mend it. Get to Sainte-Marie-de-Campan and get to the forge!"

"How far is it?"

"10 kilometres, but all downhill. No good standing there crying."

I sling the heavy bike onto my shoulder, and already it digs in. I start to walk, looking for a short cut or a fork in the road (a replacement fork? ha!) perhaps an animal path cutting across the mountainside or a broken footpath cutting across a switchback. A bike goes past, maybe two, and someone calls out in sympathy, but that is no help. I carry on down and down, every muscle aching, my shoulder bleeding, and my neck, increasingly sore and stiff. More cyclists have passed; I don't know how many (there aren't that many of us left!). How long have I been, I've lost my lead, I'll lose the race. How long have I lost—one, two hours?

On reaching Sainte-Marie, a small girl is on the roadside, she claps, "Monsieur, Bravo." Does she know where the forge is? "Oui, Monsieur," and she indicates for me to follow. In contrast to my exhausted body, I notice how light she is on her feet. Elf-like, nipping around corners and down alleys, she quickly leads me to the forge. The smithy is there and offers to mend my bike.

"No."

I turn to see a group of people that have followed me. Exhausted, I hadn't noticed.

"It is forbidden."

"What do you mean?" I exclaim.

"Any repairs to bicycles must be carried out by the cyclist."

The official is there to ensure I do not 'cheat'. I then notice the faces of managers from other teams, "Those are the rules." I know; of course, I know.

The smithy offers to tell me what to do.

"Is that allowed, I ask?" They seem unsure.

"Well, if you are unsure, it cannot be in the rules!"

"However, it cannot be done alone," adds Smithy.

Handing me a glass of wine, he explains that whilst I work, someone will need to operate the bellows to maintain the flow of oxygen and keep the temperature of the coals. A young boy, about 6 or 7 years old, offered to help, and in the heat of the forge, watched by more people than I had seen watching me cycle, I worked to mend the forks of my bike. It takes 3 hours, and I am free to go. I have lost hours of time, and yet I could punch the race official in the face when he declares, "You should not have used the child. Outside help is disallowed—I penalise you 10 minutes."

"This is supposed to be a bicycle race, the Tour de France, not an apprenticeship scheme with punishments for misdemeanours! What difference will it make? The time I have lost, I can never win back."

I guzzle back another glass of wine, pick up some bread and shove it in my pockets, climb onto my bike, and rejoin the race.

"Is there far to go? Who cares, it's no good now, we have lost."

"We're lost?" Kate asks.

At the bottom of the climb, on the left, just prior to the T junction, stands the statue of Christophe holding his broken forks aloft with a quote from him, "On abandonne jamais un travail que l'on a commence."

"You never give up a job you started." More importantly, there's a pizza restaurant right next to it.

Our stay that night was a few kilometres down the road to Campan. Our host advised that some restaurants may be closed, but there was at least a bar that did fish and chips! What followed was the now familiar disappointment and, not for the first time, an infuriating miscommunication.

We walked into town to get something to eat. (By the way, we had only shared a pizza earlier on.) As had happened in quite a few places on our journey, you could see that tourists were wandering around looking for somewhere to eat, including 3 German motorcyclists from our B&B. Nowhere was available, so we went to the bar in search of a fish and chip supper, and it was about 6.30. There was only one other person having a beer, so we were hopeful. The bar was also a store, one of those Artisanal Épicerie's that sells local and usually rather expensive produce and everything except what you actually want at that moment in time. I asked the barman if they served meals. Now, you know by now that I speak very little French; the barman spoke even less English and said that they didn't do meals. We must have looked surprised and disappointed, but that wasn't going to help. Somehow, he was able to communicate that they only did gateaux. I looked at Kate, "Well I guess we've had half a pizza. Shall we get some cake and a beer before we head back?"

We sat outside and enjoyed our beer and what was a very nice apple crumble tart. For a while, the sun even shone on us. Two of the motorcyclists, in the same predicament as us, sat down whilst their friend went back to prepare a simple meal for them made from expensive local products (that puzzled me, cheeses and cured meat? I guess it needed cutting and placing artistically on a slate.) When he was out of sight, they also ordered a beer. We shared stories about ghost towns in France that had no shops or restaurants open before talking about our trips. It was just after 7 p.m. and a couple near us had been enjoying a beer when the barman appeared and placed two plates in front of them with fish, chips, and (is there a hidden camera waiting to catch our reaction?) mushy peas! We both love mushy peas. Kate broke the stunned silence in our group, "Err, ah, oh, no, what, um…what am I missing here?" More silence, and then Kate disappears into the bar with her guide stick. About 10 minutes later, she returns to find a tandem pilot and two German motorcyclists staring, mouths open, in silence at a self-conscious couple finishing off their dinner.

"Where do I start?"

Kate explains that once inside, a woman, the English landlady, is there and asks how she can help. Kate asks if she can order a portion of fish and chips.

"Just one?"

Kate explains that we had arrived about half an hour or so ago and were informed by the barman that you only serve cake, no dinner, so we had already had something to eat. The land lady is exasperated.

"Why does he do that?" (It sounds like not the first time.)

"If you ask for a meal and it's any time before seven, he seems to think you want it immediately: he never goes on to explain when food will be available. I'll have to explain it to him—he can always call us to translate!" I stroke my stubble and look thoughtful in 'The Thinker' pose, though, unlike Rodin's sculpture, I am fully clothed. David and I had walked into a restaurant near the start of our trip to reserve a table and been told they were not open. We then went into another and had the same response, "Ce Soir?" (We asked, in unison.) "Ah, Oui," and the reservation was made…they thought we wanted to eat immediately. Have there been other occasions?

When we return to our B&B, the host (who is also English) asks us how our meal was. I explain that all the other restaurants are now closed, and the bar only does fish and chips on the first Saturday of the month between 7.03 p.m. and 7.48 p.m. unless there's a full moon.

Wow, we climbed the Tourmalet at last! Near the summit of some of these famous climbs, professional photographers wait to capture cyclists near their moment of triumph, and these are then available for purchase online later that evening or the following day. This one of Kate and I was particularly good, so after purchasing it, I posted it on the 'Voyager a velo en France' Facebook group, and it got over 400 likes and a lot of comments. Due to our near miss (fish and chips), tonight's Facebook post was later than usual, and we had several messages to check that all was well—how nice is that?

Day 34, 2nd July, distance 78.23 kilometres (3,540.64 kilometres), elevation gain 2,378m (37,258m) Depart: Campan. Arrive: Luchon.

Weather: Dry, with some pleasant 18-degree sunshine.

Food: Croissant, pain au chocolate, baguette, cereal, cake, cereal bar, sardines in tomato sauce, bread, nut mix, pancakes, lasagne, charcuterie. green salad.

La Hourquette d'Ancizan is a lesser-known (because if you're English, it's harder to pronounce or certainly more difficult to remember) Tour de France Climb that runs parallel (sort of) to the Col d'Aspin and is therefore used occasionally as an alternative. For us, it's uphill all the way, as we are at the base of the climb from the start near Campan. The climb is 21 kilometres long from here. Over this distance, the climb is less than 1,000m of climbing with an average of about 4%. Thankfully, with two more climbs to do, not a difficult climb, just long. A few years ago, we did some of today's ride in reverse, except we went over the Col d'Aspin rather than d'Ancizan.

It's nice to be able to see what this route is like and it's well worth it. Whilst riding it, we were joined by a cycle race/sportive which continued to trail behind us even after we got to the top. The front groups appear to be top amateur racers; those following are less so! The first part of the climb includes the first few kilometres (more than I had realised) of the Col d'Aspin before we turn off at Payolle, and a couple of kilometres along the road we come to a war memorial and information about the 'Combat de Payolle 10 Juillet 1944', where several local men lost their lives.

The next climb is the Col d'Azet. Again, the Col d'Azet is not one of the better-known Tour de France climbs. This climb was also not too challenging but very pretty, and the views were spectacular, with mountains and valleys to see, including the Col de Peyresourde—gulp. On our next climb, we can see across a wide, deep valley. I don't recall seeing a mountain climb across a valley so clearly. But for now, this is only a 12-kilometre climb and is consistently around 6-8%. Not so bad, eh? (Whereas the downhill felt much steeper and more technical; we were glad we were going in this direction.) There were a couple of stiffer sections, the first through the town of Azet, only about 4 kilometres in, and then near the top, a nasty 12% sting in the tail.

I now know why I put in 3 climbs today. First, in order to get to our accommodation (I find that's usually a good consideration), and second, because we joined the climb up the Col de Peyresourde already significantly up it as its start on the western side is a few kilometres down the road in Arreau, leaving us only about 8 kilometres to the top. (Mind you, we were left with the steepest section averaging 8 or 9%.) I think this was the way up that Le Tour took when Chris Froome attacked at the top and, on the way down, got onto his top bar for the best aero tuck whilst pedalling. It was very awkward and very exciting—he took about 14 seconds off his rivals, and I think he got bonus seconds as well to win the stage. It's also the perfect descent for a tandem; after a few beautiful switchbacks at the top, it's almost straight all the way down. Time to not get too overly enthusiastic and stay safe! A quick check of the brakes tells me the front is a little soft, so I'll keep it below 60kph.

At the top, we pulled into the creperie shack, a café that we had stopped at on our trip in the opposite direction back in 2016 and happened to meet some cyclists from our hometown. This time we arrived to find Bernard, and was it, Jeff? We had coffee and some crepes and shared stories since last time we met. They have also enjoyed cycling over the Tourmalet, with Jeff perhaps less so.

Towards the top of Peyresourde, we had chosen not to take a right turn. There's a ski resort called Peyragudes. The resort was only created in 1988, when the resorts of the Peyresourde and Agudes were unified. Peyragudes is accessed via the right turn a couple of kilometres below the Col de Peyresourde. It's only a few extra kilometres of climbing, and it's a climb of such significance to British cycling. The success of British cycling since 2012 is astounding, but 2012 was the first time the Tour de France was won by a Brit.

2012 was also the year of the London Olympics, and the Tour de France was in its 99th edition. It started in Belgium (even though the tour doesn't stay in France) and, of course, finished on the Champs-Élysées. The riders covered a total distance of 3,497 kilometres, and Bradley Wiggins won the overall general classification and became the first British rider to win the tour. Remarkably, Wiggins' virtually unknown teammate, Chris Froome, was second.

And the Peyragudes? Froome was leading Wiggins up the climb, and they had dropped their closest rival, Nibali. For Wiggins, this all but confirmed he would win the tour that year. (He was untouchable in the time trials and went on to win gold in the Olympics.) But what about Froome? He also had a chance of securing his place on the podium and winning another stage of the tour. It was a complex, emotional, and edgy moment to watch, with Froome wanting to push on and catch another rider up ahead without leaving Wiggins. Froome repeatedly gaps Wiggins and then waits, gesticulating perhaps impatiently for him to keep up. Wiggins, though, seems either exhausted or content. Froome either loyally remains with Wiggins or is directed to do so by the team—the stage is lost.

After our fast but safe descent with the nether regions kept well away from the top tube, we arrive in Bagnere-de-Luchon. (Bottom of the climb, where Froome may have won a stage by crushing his testicles on the top tube of his bike.) It is a Pyrenean spa town with thermal baths and a cable car up to the ski resort of Superbagneres. (Which is also a Tour de France Climb that we will not be doing as it goes in the wrong direction.)

'Luchon', I think I heard a couple of people call it, has lots of restaurants and hotels and lots to do here, especially walking in winter, skiing in summer, and gambling—either in the local casino or on the weather. Being where it is can mean there are extremes of weather, such as the 2010 storm, in which lives were lost, trees ripped from the ground, and damage to buildings and local infrastructure. Tonight was mild and pleasant, though a bit quiet as we are still ahead of the holidays.

Shortly after Kate's accident, to introduce her gently to tandem riding, we visited and cycled around the Salisbury area, where a number of places started with the name Nether, such as Nether Wallop. I referred to this as the Nether Regions. I just love the phrase, and in Chris Froome's case, Nether Wallop seems doubly appropriate.

<u>Day 35</u>, 3rd July, distance 63.21 kilometres (3,603.75 kilometres), elevation gain 1,397m (38,655m).

Depart: Luchon. Arrive: Audressein.

Weather: Low cloud am, sunny spells pm good for cycling over mountains.

Food: Croissants, baguettes, pureed apples, yoghurt, cereal, pain au raisin, boiled eggs, bread, salad, walnuts, cured meat, wildfowl, new potatoes, grilled tomatoes, and chocolate mousse.

Heading north for a number of kilometres today. We then turn to the east to head for today's mountains. In doing so, we cross the Garonne! How long ago was that? We crossed the Gironde estuary on that ferry from Royan, and the estuary is where the Garonne and the Dordogne join. The Garonne, flowing from the Spanish Pyrenees, is 529 kilometres long. It reminded me of a couple of paragraphs in 'The Rambler' (Vol 3 & 4, 1898) headed, 'Heard in the Pyrenees!': 'At a watering place in the Pyrenees, the conversation at the table turned upon a wonderful echo to be heard some distance off on the Franco-Spanish frontier.'

"It is astonishing," said an inhabitant of the Garonne. "As soon as you have spoken, you hear distinctly the voice leap from rock to rock, from precipice to precipice, and as soon as it has passed the frontier, the echo assumes the Spanish accent."

A warning though, I learnt a lesson. Yelling out at the top of my voice in English with a poor attempt at a French accent, repeatedly and then changing it to a Spanish accent might not go down well with the locals.

Col de Mente. What can you say? Only 9 kilometres; with climbs well over 20 kilometres; you can't help feeling some relief when a climb is shorter. Unfortunately, the only relief was having a pee against the sign saying it was 9 kilometres at an average of 9%. Average! I'm thinking, please, no downhills on the way. Average? We've got panniers on, let alone Kate adding an epilator, charging pack, and survival sleeping bags at the last minute! Who's even heard of this climb? (Actually, Luis Ocana.)

I will say though, the zigzags at the top are amazing, and the auberge at the top was open for coffee, perfect. Whilst enjoying that, our friend Bernard arrived through the low cloud, and we briefly caught up on our stories.

Col de Mente is on a climb with some Tour de France history regarding Luis Ocana and Eddie Merckx in 1971. The Spaniard, Ocana, was having a storming tour and had what was considered to be an insurmountable lead over Merckx. Typically, the 'Cannibal' (Merckx) was not about to give up and attacked each day, clawing back just a little time, but certainly not enough. At the Col de Mente, though, things were to dramatically changed. Merckx continued to attack, and Ocana continued to resist, but then, on a descent in torrential rain, trying to stay with Merckx, he crashed. Ocana's injuries meant that he had to abandon the tour, whilst Merckx went on to win it.

The Portet d'Aspet, I remember this climb; we have done this before in the opposite direction. (In that case, it wasn't a climb then, was it?) I recall it being quick and easy up and steep and technical down (it was in the rain), in fact not dissimilar in pain to Mente. In one sense, we were going up the harder side (steep and twisty, rising unevenly between 5 and 9% with a section touching 17%)), but it may be the safest. I recall a monument and stopping to pay respects to Fabio Casartelli, who tragically lost his life whilst descending here. It was 18th July 1995 when a few riders crashed on the descent, with Fabio's head striking concrete infrastructure on the road. Medics were at his aid within seconds, but he died in a helicopter on the journey to the hospital. A doctor argued that he would have survived if he had been wearing a helmet. From our experience, we have always believed that Kate is still alive today because of her helmet—I'll never forget putting her cracked and bloodied top of the range helmet in the bin in Tenerife. That was bloody expensive.

So, we made two tough but short climbs today, meaning that we arrived at Audressein feeling that we had achieved a lot and yet not had such a long day.

And what an ancient-looking lovely village to arrive in. The village isn't big enough to stretch your legs (much needed), but the centre of the village is delightful.

A famous woman once said, "What a lovely village" (Kate). There's a small river crossed by a bridge, or that can be crossed by a bridge and no doubt, has been crossed by a bridge—I do like a bridge, and the ones around here are quite animated. There's a quaint village centre and an unusual, eye-catching church that includes some mediaeval frescoes (I managed to get an eyebath, and hopefully all will be fine by morning.) The church has an unusual and ornate bell tower with two arches, but it is the frescoes in the porch area that require particular attention. Although they are rather faded, they can be seen more clearly if safety glasses are worn.

Our accommodation had a restaurant, but it didn't appear to be open. However, when I inquired, the landlady advised that they had a private event on, and if we were happy to eat what they were preparing for the guests, then we could be catered for. We took up the offer and had a great French three-course meal.

<u>Day 36</u>, 4th July, distance 94.78 kilometres (3,698.53 kilometres), elevation gain 2,565m (41,220m).

Depart: Audressein. Arrive: Niaux.

Weather: warm, sunny spells a.m. thunderstorms, and torrential rain p.m.

Food: Yoghurt, pain au chocolate, baguette, bread rolls, bananas, gum sweets, cheese, olives, cereal bars, mixed nuts, Tuc crackers, and bread.

Today's journey starts with a climb straight from Audressein, and it is 17.5 kilometres long. Over this distance, the climb averages 5.1% but again has irregular gradients, and it climbs 885 metres through wooded landscapes and a series of hairpins over the last few kilometres to the Col de la Core. A cyclist, Phillipe, took a photo for us. He said that he had heard from other cyclists that two English cyclists were cycling on the border of France all the way round. I said no that there were two crazy English cyclists cycling all the way round!

There are bears in the Pyrenees on the border between France and Spain, possibly about 100. Just saying. I won't mention it to Kate, unless she annoys me. Bears typically go out of their way to avoid human contact. I can't help thinking, that's if they've heard you coming. When brown bears attack, I am sure it'll be because they have been surprised.

"Okay, I don't mind you singing, but can you move on from, 'If you go down to the woods today', Please?" Kate asks.

At one point, we pass a large boulder that has fallen onto the road. As we avoid it, there are noises in the tree line. Kate asks, "What was that, did you hear it?"

"No bells, so no cows, maybe fear, er, deer?" I suggest.

It was a long, downhill from the Col de la Core. Kate said something about not rushing it and getting down nice and slow, and my mind began to wander with thoughts of Seix. When it comes to Seix, it's a matter of personal choice; you only have to search on the internet to realise that. Kate was right; there's no need to rush it; enjoy it whilst we can. Our choice was to take the right turn at Seix, adding a few more kilometres and an extra climb (I think our accommodation hosts said we couldn't arrive before 6.30 anyway.) heading for the Col de Latrape, an 18-kilometre climb. (Though averaging probably 2% for the first 12 kilometres.) At the base of the climb, we paused to track a thunderstorm that was possibly travelling across our path. I spotted it at the end of the valley to our right, and as we ate some lunch, it worked its way up and over our climb with deafening thunder and lightning. It worried Kate, but it was moving quite quickly, so we agreed to wait for it to pass.

Bernard and his friend caught us up at this point, and in glorious sunshine, they shared some local sausage and cheese with us. I took the opportunity to check on his friend's name.

"Bernard, I've forgotten your friend's name."

"It's Jean-Francoise." (Lucky, I didn't call him Jeff) "I call him Jeff; it's a lot easier."

We then left Jeff and Bernard to enjoy a break whilst we began the climb. It was fine; the descent on the other side is a steep 5 kilometres before we enter Aulus-les-Bains (the name indicating it's a thermal town) and the start of the Col d'Agne. A climb that I was expecting would be tough. (10 kilometres at an average of 8%.) We started this climb and made a few kilometres, then it darkened, and then the thunder and lightning began again. We decided to shelter for a while as it pelted it down. This time the storm didn't pass so quickly, so after about 15 or 20 minutes, just as our friends came up the climb, we decided it was better to get on with it. (It stayed with us for most of the climb.)

Leaving Aulus-les-Bains along the D8F, you very quickly realise you are not being eased into this one. My Garmin was fluctuating between 9 and 10% whilst climbing for a few slow kilometres. After about 5 kilometres, I had to check the profile to check how far there was to go; we were only about halfway. On my Garmin, I can see a series of switchbacks approaching; perhaps these will give us some respite. They do—not a lot, but enough to relieve the pressure—and they are amazing hairpins. Part of the climb has been in the forest, but as you make progress, the trees are thin and the views grow—a really satisfying climb. Cows cross the road as we near the top, where Bernard is taking a selfie next to the Col sign. Next to him, he points out to us, is a massive, muscular bull. A powerful beast that is definitely in charge of the Col. "Bye Bernard," we call as we carry on by!

Now, a little reward. A bonus, Col—an enjoyable sweeping dip down for about 3 kilometres to a lake, the Etang de Lers, and a 'quick' 3 kilometres back up, and you have conquered the Port de Lers right up top in the open.

Jeez, that was a big day—at least one climb too many and about 20 kilometres too long! Made much harder by the torrential rain up the Col d'Agne. We arrived at another hotel with a closed restaurant, and they didn't think to inform you as a staying guest! So, peanuts, TUC biscuits, a bag of grated emmental, and some tinned stuffed olives, I jest not. "…the bare necessities of life will come to you; they'll come to you! …"

Day 37, 5th July, distance 72.46 kilometres (3,770.99 kilometres), elevation gain 1,892m (43,112m).

Depart: Niaux. Arrive: Aunat.

Weather: Dry (except in the cloud at the top.)

Food: Croissant, baguette, cured sausage, honey, salted cashew nuts, gum sweets, bread, charcuterie board, cheese, small warm goat cheese salad, fillet of beef with chanterelles and ceps sauce, cheese, chocolate and custard.

About halfway through today's stage, we passed through Ax-les-Thermes, so it's a thermal town. Known for its hot springs, in particular, its bathing pool or a 'pond' right in town. The water, like all thermal baths, is purported to have healing powers and has been accessed as far back as Roman times. The springs weren't truly developed until Louis IX commissioned them in order to treat soldiers suffering from leprosy after returning from the Crusades.

The Bassin des Ladres (Lepers' Pond) is accessible on the roadside in the centre of town, and people sit around, tourists and, I assume, locals, bathing their feet. The hot springs feed the pond—it seemed very hot nearer the place the water enters the pond, and being a man, I decided it would be far too hot to sit any closer. It is very relaxing and, no doubt, very therapeutic, if only for relieving stress!

Port de Pailhères is one of only two passes in the French Pyrenees, which is over 2,000 metres altitude! I thought we were beginning to leave these damned (sorry, delightful) mountains! The other thing we have already cycled over is the Tourmalet. The climb from Ax-les-Thermes is a giant climb, almost 19 kilometres long. Over this distance, the climb is 1,281 metres, with an average gradient of 6.9% and a maximum gradient of 10.4% near the summit. The scenery is pleasant throughout; it is largely forested on the lower slopes but opens up as the switchbacks begin higher up the climb.

What really surprised us, though, was how old this road appeared and how narrow—often single-lane. Quiet (apart from a group of friendly Spanish cyclists who went up most of the way with us) and delightful (apart from a group of Spa...no only joking), it was good for keeping a comfortable snail pace. (Apart from some switchbacks somewhere that must have been about 10%, but switchbacks are always worth it.) The last 5 kilometres, though, were 9-10%, and at such a high altitude, a slog, and there was a section next to the ski resort that was as wide as a motorway—it felt like climbing a wall. This really split up the Spanish cyclists, with a couple going ahead of us and the rest struggling a long way behind. Suddenly, for the last couple of kilometres, though all the way up had been pleasant, we entered thick fog, which left you wondering exactly where the top was.

We did it, but it made the climb harder trying to see where the road meandered to the top. We then had a technical descent, steep with sharp switchbacks. that appeared to tandem riders as a slither of road twisting and plunging downwards, almost as far down as we had climbed, but more steeply. In some ways, we were thankful, but also very cautious. To start, we were in fog, then out into the sun, then through mountainside villages, oh, and in one village, we should have taken a turn. It was steep and fast down before we realised we had passed it, so we stopped and admired the view of an ancient, ruined castle on a pinnacle down the valley. We discovered a gravel and grass lane, which cut down our route at this point, so we decided to walk down it, which was probably harder work than doubling back, let alone the sound of barking dogs that seemed to encircle us. We found our road, however, ready for the final 5-kilometre climb through a beautiful and slightly scary cliffside 'balcony' road that also passed through hand-cut tunnels.

Our stopover tonight is in the tiny village of Aunat, and to get there, the road turned up a shallow valley next to some meadows and wound smoothly through some conifers down to the village in a stunning setting. We were staying in a 'pod' with its own terrace, with a view across the meadows to the hills and pine trees. After last night's nibbles, our hosts, Fabien, and Celine, gave us a great welcome, with a beer on arrival. What a great evening, lovely stay, fabulous food, and really friendly company.

Day 38, 6th July, distance 39.13 kilometres (3,810.12 kilometres), elevation gain 1,038m (44,150m).

Depart: Aunat. Arrive: Les Angles.

Weather: Pleasant; just dodged the only rain at the start of the day.

Food: Brioche, jam, cake, yoghurt, fig rolls, madeleine cake, BBQ ribs, frites, vegetables, Caesar side salad.

Today is a recovery ride. It's time to take it really easy and just spin your legs. But to begin, with Celine pointed out the rain that was travelling down the valley, so we got on the tandem and rode like the wind to get out of the valley, just slightly feeling a few raindrops as we left.

I do like bridges, but what we passed today wasn't a bridge, damn. Barrage de Puyvalador (the Puyvalador dam) is a hydroelectric dam that was built across the river Aude in the 1930s. We have spent several holidays near the Aude between here and Quillan. A great river for water sports, where we have been whitewater rafting and hydro speeding. Hydro speed involved travelling downstream in a wet suit, wearing a helmet, and holding a small board out in front, not much bigger than a float. As a man, this made me feel somewhat vulnerable, as my rocks were often dangling just over rocks and boulders by just a few centimetres as we swept down the river at speed! Mind you, the icy cold water had helped by ensuring that the undercarriage had been somewhat retracted.

We changed the front disc brake pad again (it was rattling) and surprisingly bought spares in Les Angles.

Les Angles is a ski resort, and we are staying in the summer. Having said that, it prides itself on being an authentic mountain village. Only a ski resort since the 1960s, the town has been there much longer. In the summer, the ski slopes become hiking and mountain biking destinations. It's pleasant, with lakes, Alpine meadows (bet the Pyreneans love it when you say that), and woodlands. There is plenty to do locally, including restaurants and cafés, and the local Lake Matemale and Capcir Forest cater for water sports, walks, high rope activities, mountain bike trails, and downhill rides—yet again, a place where you could spend a week or two on holiday, all year round!

In town, ski shops have become bike shops to support the cycling season. And for road cycling, road surfaces are smooth and well maintained, even though the traffic is reasonably quiet. I saw somewhere that the area is a favourite of Sylvain Chavanel for out-of-season training rides (surely all his rides are out of season these days?). Sylvain Chavanel was a combative cyclist who won 3 stages of the Tour de France in 2008 and 2010, as well as some classic races. He retired from professional cycling in 2018.

When we arrive at our accommodation each afternoon, we are never sure what it's going to be like. Consequently, I can't work out whether in that moment I am excited or apprehensive. (It feels like that when you are standing at the start of a cycling time trail.) On this occasion, I was certainly becoming apprehensive as the road out of town dropped from a nice, smooth asphalt road to an unpaved road that was gradually deteriorating. Some way ahead, we could see what appeared to be a farm building, and from the side that we approached it, it was. There was a large barn that would appear to be built for farm animals or machinery, and in front of it a fenced piece of land with numerous dogs in it that began to bark and run towards the fence. I wasn't convinced that they could not leap over it if they chose to do so. (If they were very hungry.) We were dismounted because there was a broken-up, gravel driveway that led around the corner to the front door, and lying on the driveway, lazing in the sun, was Fluffy. This was our only way to our accommodation; otherwise, I would not have led us past Fluffy. We positioned ourselves on the left side of the tandem so that it was between us and the dog, nothing like prolonging the inevitable should he attack. Fluffy just lay there, and I quietly began to sing, "The hills are alive, with the sound of music…"

"What are you doing?" asked Kate somewhat incredulously.

"I'm singing to the nice doggie."

"Couldn't we just creep past quietly?"

"Shh, you'll wake him up."

(Kate wouldn't understand. Fluffy was a monstrous three-headed dog belonging to Hagrid in the Harry Potter stories, and like Cerberus in Greek mythology, he guarded the gates to the underworld, which is evidently where we were headed. Fluffy, though, could be encouraged to fall asleep to the sound of music.)

My singing worked, and we safely reached the front door. At least I assumed it was the front door. There wasn't anything to say; there were no instructions, no welcome sign, and no doorbell. There were children's toys lying around on the ground amongst the dog excrement. I knocked a few times, waited at least a minute, then tried again. Nothing. I opened the door because I could see it led into a porch and stepped inside. There were some tables against the wall with half-dead plants growing out of pots and growing bags. On one table, there was an envelope with 'Bosley' pencilled on it. I reached forward to collect it, and what seemed like dozens of flies flew up into my face as apprehension shot down from my frown straight through and into my bib shorts. Nonetheless, gathering myself, I triumphantly exited the porch holding the retrieved envelope aloft like Indiana Jones with the treasure and the bag of sand (just before he realises it's a trap and the tomb is about to collapse.)

"Treasure!" I announce to Kate. I explained that there is no one around, so I'll go in and check it out.

I breathe in deeply and hold my breath so that I can get through the porch without swallowing any flies. I then go through a door into a very dark hallway; it's so dark that I must wait for my eyes to become accustomed to it. (As well as my reactive sunglasses.) I find our room and cautiously enter it. On the right is a door into a bathroom; straight ahead is a window looking out at a gorgeous view with a forest, a lake, and mountains, and the first thing I really notice is the clean white sheets on the pine bed. I go to get Kate.

"It's not great, but it'll be okay."

"It's all a bit weird, but it'll do," agreed Kate. Whilst Kate goes for a shower, I close the windows, which have been left open and have allowed quite a few flies into the bedroom.

Kate then calls, "There are no toiletries," and that was just the start. I then notice that the linen and towels feel damp (they look and smell okay); then there's the damp, slippery bathroom floor, which remained so for the whole stay. I prefer not to think about that.

We managed to find a place to eat in town and even arranged for a bike workshop to give the tandem a safety check in the morning. We arrived back to the dogs, and Fluffy somehow, feeling unclean, went to bed. We still talk about this place, and why didn't we leave and find an alternative? I subsequently checked the reviews for the place, and they are not that bad at all, but one stood out that was left about a month after our visit.

Stayed in August 2023 Perhaps we should have gotten a medal or a T-shirt for staying.

Day 39, 7th July, distance 120.39 kilometres (3,930.51 kilometres), elevation gain 1,484m (45,634m).

Depart: Les Angles. Arrive: Amelie.

Weather: Sunny, 26 degrees, very pleasant, like a holiday.

Food: Croissants, pain au chocolate, fruit puree, fig rolls, mixed nuts, charcuterie, burgers, frites.

Still no sign of the hosts we located the breakfast room, which also appeared unsavoury, grabbed our croissant and pain au choc (thankfully they were still in the paper bag from the shop), and left.

By 9 a.m., we were sitting outside the DH Ecobike eating our breakfast in the sun whilst the mechanic checked over, tuned up, and replaced the rear tyre, a brake pad, and a new chain. That felt reassuring, as we had no rest days planned until the end of the Alps.

We were back on the road within an hour. After a few kilometres on beautiful roads and past a couple of pretty lakes, we had a short but nice climb up the Col de la Llosa, followed by a 24-kilometre-long technical downhill. In my mind, this was a transition day to get us out of the mountains, but that sometimes makes you overlook what the day is like. This was an amazing route, where you could see the road zigzagging way down below through gorges and along the sides of valleys. Also, another glorious day. Spirits weren't dampened, even when we got our first rear wheel puncture—on the new tyre, by Sod's law, of course.

I made a note to check out the Chateau Castell d'Evol. It's an ancient and mythical place dating as far back as the twelfth century. I failed to check it out, and later I discovered it's a long walk from the road. We could have cycled to Evol to see it, but it was 3-4 hours away, supposedly—so it remains a mythical castle!

The biggest climb of the day, the Col de Palomere, is 22 kilometres long but averages only 3.5% (max 8). I think the Pyrenees are running out of strength. But it did drag on a bit in the heat of the day; we've not become accustomed to all this nice weather. It was then a long, fast descent downhill to today's finish at Amelie-Les-Bains-Palalda with its narrow streets, pleasant river, and hot spring baths. (Or in our case, a nice shower in a clean and pleasant apartment.) As it was an apartment, we had a washing machine—a chance to get everything clean and dry and go out for a nice meal.

Day 40, 8th July, distance 121.84 kilometres (4,052.35 kilometres), elevation gain 534m (46,168m).

Depart: Amelie. Arrive: Prat de Cest.

Weather: Sunny, 27 degrees, some breeze, but warming right through the body like a gentle massage.

Food: Fig rolls, croissants, baguettes, emmental, Niçoise pizza, cereal bars, kebabs, goats cheese salads.

Over 4,000 kilometres ridden now, shouldn't we be tired? If the plan works, no. We are past halfway and we continue to ride at a pace and distance that we know we can comfortably achieve—it seems to be working. (So far).

Downhill to the sea, and today's profile was not like any other on the trip so far. It looked like the profile of a bath from the end, where you rest your head all the way down and along, to just before the plug hole, which, in this bath, is at your feet. (I have always had difficulty with analogies.) I imagined letting go of the soap at the head end and watching it slide all the way along, and I hoped the ride would be that frictionless!

The first point of any significance was just where the bath curved, which was at the Port-Argelès on the Mediterranean! At the foot of the Albères mountains, just at the place where the Pyrenees plunge down to the sea, is the village of Argelès-sur-Mer, with a wonderful stretch of beach and a picturesque port at the southern end. We immediately found a café on the beach and celebrated with coffee and a croissant.

Having slid along the coast past Perpignan, we are now slipping along just under the backs of your knees (do they have a name?) at a place called Le Barcares. This was the starting point of our somewhat easier Pyrenean ride a few years ago. I remember that it had giant flowerpots on the roadside, and I took a photo of David apparently holding one in his hand.

I must mention Port Leucate, which we struggled to pass with about 20 kilometres to go somewhere along the chain-tattooed calf muscle. Port Leucate is in a homonymous town. That's it; I need to say no more about the place. I got to use the word homonymous.

And finally, like the soap hardly losing momentum, we slip into the plug hole beside the Chateau Prat de Cest just before Narbonne—a lagoon. The plug hole is rather more attractive than expected without pubic hair in sight.

By the way, no doubt you know. Homonymous can mean that if two words are described as such, then they are homonyms. That is, words that have a different meaning but are pronounced or spelt the same, for example; plug (electrical) and plug (bath plug). Get an unforgettable example of this; search for The Two Ronnies (Fork Handles sketch!). In this, a customer enters a hardware store and appears to ask for "four candles." Once the impatient shopkeeper has found these, the customer says, "No, fork handles, handles for forks."

The customer then requests, "plugs."

"Right, what kind of plugs?" Checks the shopkeeper, determined not to be caught out this time.

"A rubber one, bathroom."

The shopkeeper thinks he knows what's wanted and, after a lengthy search, returns with a box of rubber bath plugs but doesn't know what size the customer needs.

"What size?"

"Thirteen amp." And so the sketch continues.

Having said that, in this instance, homonymous means having the same name, so forget the plug story! (Bloody English language!)

I mentioned that we struggled to pass Port Leucate. There is a bridge there—the only bridge that enables you to cross towards Leucate that we needed to cross, but we did have trouble finding how to get on it. It is one of those infuriating situations where road infrastructure does not favour cyclists. At one point, we ended up underneath the bridge, down by the water's edge, but the road leading up and over the bridge was built up like a flyover. Eventually, we traced the road back a few kilometres until we could join the busy traffic.

Inevitably, as we crossed the bridge, we found ourselves on a busy narrow lane, and a cycle path appeared on the right across concrete dividers—the route we had been looking for. Thankfully, we could eventually get across to it after a few minutes, which was worthwhile for the great views of the lagoon on one side and the port on the other, as well as a greater sense of safety. These things can take a lot of time and are frustrating in the heat of the day. We lost about an hour and added about 8 kilometres.

All forgotten, though, when we arrive at the accommodation and get taken to a room big enough to have 2 double sliding windows looking out and another to the side, a swimming pool, and free soft drinks…recovery time. The restaurant is not nearby, but the host very kindly ordered pizzas on our behalf, to be delivered!

Day 41, 9th July, distance 135.81 kilometres (4,188.16 kilometres), elevation gain 373m (46,541m).

Depart: Prat. Arrive: Palavas-Les-Flot.

Weather: Glaring sun, max 34 degrees, little breeze, whatever you do, don't get a puncture out in the open, especially not a rear wheel puncture.

Food: Brioche, croissants, toast, apricots, baguettes, bread rolls, tuna, soup de poisson, chicken, rice, Café Gourmand.

The Mediterranean coast means incredibly flat cycling for a few days. What did I do? Rather than think, bonus, relax, I only went and upped the distance, and what did global warming do? Brought a heatwave!

Leaving Prat, we head straight for the coast but have a couple of false starts to avoid sandy, gravelly tracks that we really don't want to get stuck down. Gruissan, an old village that stands out amongst the sea and lagoons, is the first place we come to, overlooked by the mediaeval tower of Barberousse, all that remains of a castle from the 10th century. The castle was intended to be an outlook against invaders and guard Narbonne against any seaborne attacks. It was destroyed in the 16th century and has been left in ruins ever since. The town is circular, surrounding the castle, so I plotted a route around the outline of the town for fun.

As well as its village with cute little streets, there are two marinas and a very nice nearby beach. Our route didn't take us close to the resort of Gruissan-Plage, but its picturesque neighbourhood, made up of 1,300 chalets on stilts, sounds amazing! Shortly after, we travelled a few kilometres inland to find a bridge over the Aude, now having travelled from its source in Les Angles to where it joins the Mediterranean Sea. Then back inland again to get to Sérignan, to find a bridge to get over the Orb river. It's a hot day, but the good roads mean that we are travelling at a steady pace, which creates its own cooling breeze.

We then arrived at the Etang de Thau. This was such a big lake; we seemed to be cycling on a thin strip of land between the lake and the sea for ages, about 20 kilometres. This becomes a regular theme until the Alps. The Bassin de Thau is the largest of a string of lagoons that stretch along the French coast from the Rhône River to the foothills of the Pyrenees that we cycled past, around, and occasionally through (Etang du Vic coming up!).

First, though, is the Canal du Rhône à Sète, which is exactly what it says on the tin. It's a canal that connects the Étang de Thau in Sète to the Rhône River in Beaucaire. The canal is made up of two pre-existing canals, the Canal des Étangs and Canal de Beaucaire. These waterways are amazing, and this canal also connects with the Canal du Midi by virtue of the fact that they both join the Étang de Thau. Cycling along this coast provides such a contrast, with new and equally beautiful things to see compared to other parts of France. The jostling and busy parts of the route are worth it.

Our destination for today and the odd-looking place on the map is Palavas-les-Flots, a seaside town just a few kilometres south of Montpellier. But we have to get to it, and it's on the other side of the Etang du Vic. I have spotted something that fills me with a sense of dread, but I can't resist the intrigue. The Canal du Rhone a Sete passes across or within the lake. Kate agrees; we just have to investigate. We went to a bridge over the canal at Frontignan Plage, and what a stunning view! A wide canal stretches off into the distance. Inland has the canal wall and a thin stretch of scrub land; on the other side, it is very similar, but a gravel track seems to travel along it. To the left and right is the lake that it is passing through. It's a long way off in the distance, probably about 15 kilometres, so we can just pick out the buildings at our destination. Can this be done? Is it allowed? A Frenchman is walking over the bridge with his family.

"Excusez-moi, parlez-vous Anglais?"

"Non, seulement quelques mots." I take it that he doesn't and point into the distance, "Palavas?"

"Yes, Palavas-les-Flots."

I then point to the gravel track below, "Et ici, est-ce un Piste Cyclable?"

"Yes, c'est, ça va à Palavas-Les-Flot." I need to check, "we can cycle there?"

"Oui, yes, you go." I thank him, and he can see that we are pleased to see this, "Bon voyage."

That's it then. Back down from the bridge, onto the track, and off we go. The track doesn't appear too bad, though, definitely the type of track I intended to avoid. Very soon, occasional cyclists pass us in the opposite direction, which is encouraging, but a couple of kilometres in and we realise that this is going to be a long journey! It remains an amazing experience, though. Along the way, there is an occasional gap in the road where the canal and surrounding lake are joined. (Water can enter the canal from the lake.) Here, short, narrow bridges allow you to continue your journey.

Unfortunately, with only a few kilometres to go, it was one of those bridges that made the day significantly harder. As we accelerated to get up and over one of these bridges, the rear wheel thudded against the edge (in effect, the bridge had been placed on the track by a crane, I expect, without any material to provide a smooth transition onto it, just a sharp edge), and we suffered what is known as a pinch puncture. That is, rather than a puncture caused by a sharp object piercing the inner tube, it's when you hit a sharp edge hard with your bike tyre and it presses and pinches your inner tube against your rim hard enough to puncture the tube. We were now stationary, 35 degrees in the shade, with no breeze. Basically, not the time to hesitate.

We removed the luggage and the rear wheel and quickly changed the inner tube before replacing everything. Sweat was dripping from my forehead and chin onto the tyre as I coaxed it back onto the wheel. A bit of relief, but very keen to reach our destination we set off again and perhaps made 500 metres before we had a second puncture and rear wheel again. Kate was not happy; usually comfortable in the heat, she was exasperated that a second puncture should happen. We were near a small bush that provided just enough shade for her to rest in whilst I went through the process again. This time I was more careful to check that there was not a sharp object embedded in the tyre, that the tyre wasn't damaged, or that I wasn't catching the inner tube as I refitted the tyre. This time I was so hot that beads of sweat covered my arms and legs and were stinging my eyes. But job done, we were back on our way. It's amazing how the motion of the bike can provide a cooling breeze, so it was a great relief to get going. I was anxious for the rest of the journey on that path, but no further problems arose.

The main centre of Palavas-les-Flots lies along the edges of the river Lez on a section that has been developed into a canal just before it enters the sea. These canals and waterways are so intricate and interconnected. A lot of the time, I'm thinking ahead as to whether we'll be having to turn back, wade across, or just leap over a dyke, but there is nearly always a bridge. The river splits the town, and along the edges of the canal there are bars and restaurants, making it perfect for greedy and thirsty cyclists. In the centre of the town is the 'lighthouse of the Mediterranean', with a revolving restaurant designed to aid the digestive system (maybe).

It's not the type of place I'd recommend to anyone for a holiday, but it is unusual, and it's nice to have seen it. That's always one of the advantages of cycling, you see things that may be hidden, and you never know what's around the corner. There is also a concrete pier from which you get some good views of Palavas-les-Flots and out across the bay to La Grande Motte—easy to recognise for its whacky triangular-shaped buildings that we will pass through in the morning.

We had a shower, some fluids, and a great meal out. It's remarkable how quickly you can recover.

Day 42, 10th July, distance 130.62 kilometres (4,318.78 kilometres), elevation gain 189m (46,730m) Depart: Palavas-Les-Flot. Arrive: Port-de-Bouc.

Weather: Hot, 37 degrees, so make sure to have plenty of fluids and keep to decent roads, and lots of shade!

Food: Croissant yoghurt fruit salad, toast, baguettes, egg, brioche, gel, milkshake, charcuterie, salmon pasta.

Another long day in the saddle and yet more lakes, including the Etang de L'Or. It's another strange-looking thing on my route plan, in this instance where we appear to cycle on the narrowest of roads or paths between lake and sea, and I do have a sense of unease about what the path might be like, so much so that I play safe and share my unease with Kate. Kate now has a sense of unease. I tell her to stop worrying; what's the worst that could happen? The wildlife reserve is as close to Montpelier as you can get. Possibly one of the reasons that Montpellier is where it is by providing local access to food sources, salt, and windsurfing.

Just after the lake is Le Grau-du-Roi, a village that has beaches on the Med, but salt marshes and a mediaeval port (Aigues-Mortes) are immediately behind it. It is very hot, and we are most comfortable when we are cycling, so we do.

The port is worth visiting with its mediaeval walls surrounding the town, but I am beginning to get a little apprehensive about the next part of today's route.

We arrive at Saintes-Maries-de-la-Mer, a holiday resort on the coast, sandwiched between lakes and nature reserves. Somewhere here, I'm hoping there's a cycle path that enables us to continue our journey across this wild part of the Camargue. If we can't go this way, then we have probably got a 30-kilometre detour to make. (Possibly a few kilometres less, but my numeral keys for five and six aren't working. I will prise them up and give them a blow later!) Where is this path? My planned route takes us to a barrier blocking the entrance to a campsite. We track around the campsite via residential roads until we come to what appears to be a coastal path, but after about 499 metres, it is covered in sand, blowing off the sand dunes. There's a side entrance to the campsite, and I wonder whether the path passes through the site. A couple of security guards are at the gate. They don't speak English, "Ou-est la Piste Cyclable, Ici?"

"Non, a l'entrée principale a gauche." Having thanked them, we head back to the main gate, where there's a small road on the left over a dyke and a gravel road running through some wasteland. It's just something we didn't want to do, but perhaps it'll travel around the campsite and then join an asphalt superhighway. At least 24.99 kilometres later, we at last joined an asphalt road. The gravel road had become a footpath that, to begin with, had a few sections covered with sand. We wouldn't have continued from this point, but a woman pushing a fully laden, touring bike, followed by at least two children pushing their own bikes, came in the opposite direction through the sand, and without being asked, to let us know that there were only two or three short sand sections, which was really thoughtful. We had passed some salt beds before reaching the edge of the lake, which opened up before us, "John, look left: aren't those flamingos?"

Nearby, there must have been 40 or 49 flamingos in a shallow Salt Lake, but as you looked at the scene, you began to realise that there were thousands of them as far as the eye could see. Flamingos stop at the lake because, as part of the Camargue region, it is a large wetland area that provides them with food, shelter, and breeding grounds. It is also close to the Parc Ornithologique de Pont de Gau, a bird sanctuary where flamingos can be observed and protected. This year, a record-breaking 60,000 flamingos flocked to the Camargue region, and it was a spectacular sight. This was worth seeing, even though it did mean, for the second day running, that the cycling was particularly challenging. (Who needs mountains?) We now had kilometres after kilometres of salt lakes and lagoons with rough, gravel tracks to ride over. This is whilst a heatwave is hitting the area; there is no breeze and no shade, and we are low on fluids. (One bidon left between us.)

After a number of kilometres, I can see ahead the colour of the rough gravel change to what looks like tarmac, and I foolishly let Kate know that we were heading for a paved road, but no, we now find ourselves riding on a surface that's like cinder or pumice and looks even more likely to give us a puncture. There are still amazing sights, though, some lakes that have dried up and just have a salt-covered bed, and then a spectacular lighthouse, the Phare de Faraman. It is an unmanned lighthouse and has black and white stripes like a zebra crossing. Except for going upwards, you cannot cross it.

In 1934, the smooth masonry was painted with six alternating horizontal black and white stripes. It was restored during the late 40s, due to damage suffered in the Second World War. In 1972, it received a wind turbine, was automated, is now powered by electricity, and remains unmanned.

The south coast of France is conveniently divided into two parts: west of the Rhone (Languedoc) and east of the Rhone (Provence—Riviera). This just makes things much simpler for my brain to take in. Languedoc offers miles upon miles of flat sandy seashores—this is the Mediterranean, so they aren't wide (or that deep), but the almost non-existent tide and waves do not encroach upon them significantly. (Unlike on the Atlantic Coast, where you have to stifle your laughter as sun worshippers, along with their towels and belongings, get caught out and dragged into the sea.) Of course, the water is warmer here as well.

At Arles, the Rhone River divides into the Grande Rhône and the Petit Rhône. The resulting delta forms the Camargue region, where we continue to travel across and, out of fluids, we now look towards the next town. We need to get across a few more kilometres of gravel, then possibly only 4–10 kilometres to a ferry crossing next to which is Salin-de-Giraud. I know that Kate is struggling with the lack of fluid, so I'm anxious to get somewhere. Dehydrated, sweaty, and tired, we finally join a perfect asphalt road and dig deep to get quickly to the ferry with a quick detour into the town. We do quite quickly find three potential places to get fluids; two are closed, but we pull up outside a restaurant where a woman is sat under a canopy at a smoking table.

Behind her, through a slatted fence, I can see people eating under a canopy and having drinks on their tables. As we park the tandem, she asks what we would like, and Kate asks for two glasses of coke, and two coffees. I can see that the woman is beginning to deny Kate's request, so I interject and explain that we need some fluids and would also like to buy some water. The response is defiant and finally negative, "This is my restaurant; it is not a bar." In that moment, I had just met the evilest woman in France and just stared at her. I should have challenged her further, but I was convinced there would be somewhere on the ferry; that was a mistake; there was not. (The ferry was crossing the Rhone at Le Bac de Barcarin.)

After the ferry crossing, we cycled a couple of kilometres to a T junction, which our route ignored, and went straight on down another gravel track below a series of wind turbines that disappeared into the distance. (A little note was now logged somewhere in my brain at this point; it read, 'Never mind your intentions; switch to gravel tyres for your next big tour.') We checked the route and could see that over the next few kilometres, if we could just get past this gravel section, there were two or three places where we should get fluids. We were both beginning to struggle now. Progress was so slow, but finally we got back onto the road for what seemed like an age.

The roads had become busy with large commercial vehicles, and although there was a wide shoulder to cycle along, they had become unpleasant. Quite quickly though we turned into what turned out to be an extensive commercial zone, not a town or village with large container lorries and warehouses, about ¾ of an hour later, we despondently came back out at the point we had entered, slowing and exhausted. We decided to just aim for Fos-sur-Mer and pedalled on. The traffic changed to cars and holiday traffic—then, after about ½ hour, we approached a roundabout. Kate spotted it, "Next right, McDonalds!" Never had we been so pleased to see a McDonald's.

We grabbed a seat outside in the shade. (Upper 30s, but a little breeze helped.) Kate removed her guide stick from the frame of the tandem and went in to order fluids; she returned laughing, "I may have over done it." She ordered 3 large cokes, 2 large lattes, and 2 milkshakes. "We can put anything left in our bottles." All good, almost, but the French don't do fast food. I'm now in a bit of a state, and this has happened to me before, I keep going when I'm on the bike, but when I stop, exhaustion, whether caused by heatstroke, dehydration, or hunger (possibly all of them), starts to take over. Every minute that passes, I have to take deeper breaths to cope with the dizziness and nausea that are creeping up on me. "Where are they?" I don't know how long they have taken; it seems like about 20 minutes, but I must go and lay on the grass next to the tandem, partly to recover and partly in case I need to throw up.

Kate keeps checking on me, "Are you okay?" and I impatiently say yes because the effort interrupts my breathing and makes me feel worse. I begin to regain control, and the nausea fades. I can see the drinks have arrived, but get up slowly because I know I'll be unsteady. A few sips of the milkshake first, not too much as the cold might not be good, then some gulps of the nice, refreshing Pepsi, not too much in case it's too fizzy, followed by some sips of the coffee, not too much in case it's too hot. You can see I've already decided I'm drinking a lot, and I'm in no rush. Kate is already looking a lot happier (I decided to go into the next room, where there is a big daddy bed, a middle-size mummy bed).

We must have been there for the best part of an hour, and all the drinks were gone. We have the last few kilometres of our ride to do; we can just take it easy and feel so relieved that it's over and we can ride gently down the cycle path. No, actually, we can't. We turn to cycle along the Canal de Fos a Bouc, and it's a broken-up gravel carpark with 3 totally demoralising kilometres of potholes, gravel, and dust. We made it, of course, and the room was perfectly nice, though we didn't enjoy the evening meal down by the harbour. What is there to say about Port-de-Bouc? It's a pleasant and busy fishing harbour and fish market. It did look as though people could buy fish directly from the fishermen, or, with their eye patches and parrots on their shoulders, perhaps there was something else on sale. You can't escape the industrial landscape, though; it's not a place I'd recommend for a holiday. We just needed fluids and rest.

Day 43, 11th July, distance 73.40 kilometres (4,392.18 kilometres), elevation gain 689m (47,419m).

Depart: Port-de-Bouc. Arrive: Cassis.

Weather: Humid 29 degrees, it could be hot on the climb later on.

Food: Croissants, pain au chocolate, yoghurt, fruit puree, baguette, puree pouch, gel sweets, soup de poisson, entrecôte, potatoes, Mediterranean veg, pear tart.

Up and breakfasted, and you wouldn't even know what we'd gone through the day before—particularly considering the previous day was also tough. We both knew what we had in store was not going to lift the spirits until the afternoon, but by then we'd have had some tough cycling out of the way. We also both agreed that it had been worth doing, this route for the unusual things we saw. The ride from Port-de-Bouc to Port-de-Marseille doesn't really need much description; it was often on large roads with infrequent cycle lanes, but it got us there. The main difficulties were when you hit a multitude of roads at the Port of Marseille. It becomes very difficult to watch the road and watch out for signs indicating cycle routes. Consequently, at times we were in cycle lanes that presumably turned off at a junction because we would very quickly not be on one. However, it was more inconvenient and stop-and-go than a sense of danger. There must be better routes through, though, if you are not trying to cycle near the coast. Once we had navigated through it, it all changed.

The Parc National des Calanques is an area of outstanding natural beauty, with rugged landscapes, cliffs, hidden bays, and extensive routes for walking and mountain biking. The park spans about 20 kilometres of coastline between Marseille and Cassis and is unusual for being the only European national park to encompass land, sea, and urban areas.

Our route from the outskirts of Marseille to Cassis only took about an hour or so and included our first climb, since the Alps, the Col de la Gineste. It's a spectacular climb as it climbs out of Marseille for a couple of kilometres before sweeping back into a wide arc so that you have commanding views of Marseille and its port. It's about 5 kilometres long and steady between 4–6%.

In the heart of the Calanques National Park, Cassis, our resting place today, paints a picture of life in a Provencal fishing village. It's a lovely place for walking, with pastel-coloured houses lining the quaint harbour, charming shops and cafes for tourists, sand/shingle beaches (I'm sure it was pebbles last time I was here!), and beautiful views of the French Riviera and its bright blue waters. Kate and I had visited here before we were even married. It was nice to come back—a few thousand other visitors had the same idea.

Day 44, 12th July, distance 67.42 kilometres (4,459.60 kilometres), elevation gain 897m (48,316m).

Depart: Cassis. Arrive: Toulon.

Weather: Same as yesterday, which was quite pleasant.

Food: Fruit puree, choc chip brioche, mixed nuts, fruit cake, Mentos (fruit), choc chip brioche! Salad de Chèvre; cheeseburger, salad, frites.

The day started by climbing up out of Cassis on the Route de Crete, averaging about 13% and maxing out around 17%. That soon in the morning, climbing can be a shock, but we know that we can start cycling by taking it steady and pushing harder when particularly steep sections need it, recovering when they don't. It's a beautiful route, and it eventually turns out to be a lot easier and a lot more spectacular than we had expected. One of those rides where, at any given moment, one of us is saying, "Wow!"

Between Cassis and La Ciotat are the Soubeyranes cliffs, including, at almost 400 metres, the highest seaside cliff in France. Shaped by wind erosion, the landscape is interesting, with bays and inlets, unusual rock formations, and new sights around every corner. Due to yet another road closure, we had to miss out on one of the headlands (Les Hautes Leques), knocking at least 10 kilometres off our ride.

I have a tendency to want to finish the day past a city if there is one in the way, so that we don't start the day going through one, and Toulon today was no exception. This isn't always great when you are getting tired and have to get through a city, but the day turned out to be shorter than planned. In this instance, it also looked like we'd missed the opportunity to stay in a nice coastal city lined with sandy beaches and shingle coves. It's both a naval base; the harbour is home to submarines and warships, and a fishing harbour, with fishing boats and ferries. It's a lesson about not being so rigid in my behaviour, and one that I'll undoubtedly ignore because that's what rigid behaviour is about, ignoring alternatives and consequently missing potentially rich life experiences. I wonder what I've been missing. Of course, the fact that I don't know means I haven't missed anything.

Day 45, 13th July, distance 121.62 kilometres (4,581.22 kilometres), elevation gain 863m (49,179m).

Depart: Toulon. Arrive: Frejus.

Weather: 32 degrees; the temperature is just pushing back up again, but the hills look gentle.

Food: Pain au chocolate; croissants; cereal; fruit cocktail; yoghurt; baguettes; eggs; mentos; mixed nuts; Salad Nicoise; Moussaka.

This is a rocky, jagged coast characterised by small inlets, shingly or sandy beaches, and spectacular landscapes. A lot of the beaches here seem to be of shingle or fine pebbles, including the famous beach beside the seafront at Nice—I can remember being there on holiday and some people being disappointed that it wasn't dry, sand-timer type sand. I have mixed feelings, though. It feels clean on pebbles, and at least you don't get itchy skin and gritty sandwiches. This is the region with the most famous French seaside resorts—Saint Tropez, Saint Raphael, Cannes, Nice, and many others. It is an area that is extremely popular in the summer. As for the 'best beaches in France', that's really a matter of individual choice.

The first 40 kilometres of today's ride were along amazing Piste Cyclables and, when necessary, cycle lanes—very easy cycling that got us out of Toulon quickly, safely, and enjoyably. We then did have a few climbs, but very gentle gradients. The most significant climb started at La Croix-Valmer, a fun, winding little climb that was only about 3 kilometres long with an average gradient of 3% and a maximum of 6%, quite pleasant, called the Col de Collebasse.

About two-thirds into today's ride, we passed through Saint-Tropez, a coastal fishing port on the French Riviera, where unnecessarily expensive-looking yachts seem to outnumber fishing boats. We didn't linger; it was a bottleneck with very slow traffic, so we quickly moved on.

Shortly after, we reached Port Grimaud, a well-known coastal town that has only been in existence for around fifty years. (The port, not the village.) It's a colourful port, and it's no surprise that it's nicknamed 'The Little Venice of Provence' with its canals and waterside buildings, one of which a WC has scribbled on its door, 'The little Penis of Provence'. (Well, it does now.) The village of Grimaud is a perched village (village perché) dominated by an 11th-century castle.

Frejus is similarly pleasant and somewhat cheaper to stay in than Saint-Tropez or Port Grimaud, so guess where we stayed. Fréjus is a port town with Roman ruins, including an amphitheatre, a theatre and aqueduct, and a gothic cathedral.

My keyboard now has a missing number five key, and neither that nor number six work. I have discovered that the days of giving something a whack and it working again are long gone. Perhaps something to also tell my osteopath.

Day 46, 14th July, distance 71.74 kilometres (4,652.96 kilometres), elevation gain 487m (49,666m).

Depart: Frejus. Arrive: Cagnes-Sur-Mer.

Weather: 29 degrees, so I took it easy.

Food: Croissants, fruit salad, yoghurt, pain au chocolate, egg, baguettes, bananas, Neapolitan pizza.

It's another reasonably flat day today, but with a climb up to La Corniche d'Or, the road that connects Saint-Raphaël to Cannes. It was opened in 1903 with the support of the 'Touring Club of France' providing beautiful views of the coastline. with lots of little bays and numerous tunnels and curved viaducts for the train line to traverse the hills and valleys. It's spectacular, but it is an easy day, ready for a big day tomorrow when we turn left into the Alps!

Cannes—you can't really cycle through without mentioning it. (If ever proof were needed.) The extremes that you see cycling around France! Cannes is probably best known for its international film festival. Its main promenade (Boulevard de la Croisette) curves along the edge of its sandy beach, with its expensive boutiques and grand hotels facing opposite.

Then we cycled on to Antibes, sort of a downmarket Cannes, but also a finish for the Raid Alpine, which we completed in about 2015. The Raid Alpine starts in Thonon-Les-Bains, which we will be passing through, next to Lac Leman (also known as Lake Geneva) and ends 740 kilometres later in Antibes. When I look back on it, I can't believe that we completed that on a tandem, and I remind myself so I can see how manageable the Alps should be this time! The route of the Raid Alpine was designed by Georges Rossini and climbs over more than 30 cols. (Many used for the Tour de France.) As an official Randonnée, a medal is awarded to anyone who completes it within the time limit—which I recall is 100 years, no, hours, I think. More details of that trip are on the Snails around France Facebook page.

Our destination today is near Nice, at Cagnes-Sur-Mer. In the 1919 Tour de France, Eugene Christophe (our cycling hero whose forks broke on the Tourmalet a few years earlier whilst digging into a pizza) passed this way, leading the race for the 5th stage in a row, and by the end of tomorrow's stage (Nice to Grenoble), 'Tour' history was made when he was still in the lead and was awarded the first ever 'maillot jaune' (yellow jersey), which he would hold onto for 4 more stages. Desperate bad luck would strike again for Christophe. On the penultimate stage, still in the lead, between Metz and Dunkerque, his forks would again break whilst riding over cobbles. He again found a forge and repaired his bike, finishing third (overall) in Paris. It can be a cruel sport.

Tomorrow, we head into the Alps, and it's an area we don't know, which makes us fear that we may have a similar experience to those ludicrously steep roads into the Pyrenees. We had a good look at the profiles of the climbs that we would be doing tomorrow, and, though long, they don't look beyond our comfort zone. The bits we can't see are bits in between, short ascents leading to the climbs. We'll just take that as it comes—and if there are very steep bits, they can only be short, I think. Kate, "You think?" The, 'I think' is never totally reassuring!

Day 47, 15th July, distance 90.06 kilometres (4,743.02 kilometres), elevation gain 2,393m (52,059m).

Depart: Cagnes-Sur-Mer. Arrive: Col de Turini.

Weather: 37 degrees, which is rather hot for mountain climbing, so we got up early. I don't do early very well.

Food: Croissants, breakfast biscuits, pureed apples, bread rolls, sardines, croissants, cereal bars, charcuteries, mushroom omelettes, frites, and baguettes.

I know this feeling, the one where you often think it's nervousness when it's adrenaline, or apprehension rather than excitement. It's all of these. There are a few places we'll need to concentrate on that may be busy and difficult to navigate. (We have to get around Monaco.) But ultimately, it's the turn into Alps with some significant climbs that's probably the most exciting part. Over 2,300m of climbing in a heatwave requires a change of tactics and a different approach from our usual style. (Again, do we have a usual style anymore?)

- First, we chose to set off early 6.30 a.m. This meant cooler, quieter, quicker, and absolutely beautiful. (That does not mean I'm making a habit of it!)
- Take fluids on board early, from the start, even if it's only a little sip, and make sure the bidons are full when we turn left at Menton.
- Regularly rest in the shade rather than attempting to complete the climbs without stopping.
- It's not a race; act like a snail and enjoy it.

By the end of today, we will be climbing high into the Alps. This will be a challenge, but I have to mention the author and cyclist, Elizabeth Robins Pennell. Pennell (1855–1936) and her husband Joseph began cycling in the 1870s first on a tandem trike and later on safety bicycles. (Bicycles that were very similar in design to today's bikes.) They travelled by bicycle extensively, with Pennell writing books and articles and Joseph illustrating them. "There is no more healthful or more stimulating form of exercise; there is no physical pleasure greater than that of being borne along, at a good pace, over a hard, smooth road by your own exertions." "Over the Alps on a Bicycle," was published in 1898 and documented their journey through some of the highest Alpine passes in Europe. These were very basic bicycles on roads, no more than gravel tracks.

What an incredible woman! So, no complaints; this really should be comfortable really!

First things first is Monaco in France? Monaco is officially the Principality of Monaco and is a sovereign state. Widely recognised as one of the most expensive and wealthiest places in the world, is a good enough reason for us not to enter, as well as not wishing to break our rule of not entering another country.

Here you go, Cornwall, a sovereign state! That reminds me, does anyone fancy a Fisherman's Friend? "I used to, but I married him, and that all changed."

Fisherman's Friends are strong menthol lozenges that, like snails, you either love or hate them and there's a French connection. French President Emmanuel Macron has apparently favoured Fisherman's Friends, keeping them to hand when he is public speaking.

From Zero to Hero today, from sea level and up to the Col de Turini. You just turn left and start going up!

First up is Col de Castillon. (15 kilometres, averaging 5%.) Once you've negotiated the main road out of Menton and passed the turn-off to the motorway (which was straightforward), the road becomes a lot quieter and more scenic. It's a steady gradient, nothing too strenuous, but once past the first village of Monti, it is relentless in the heat, and it is wonderful. At one point in the distance, you can see an impressive arched viaduct on the mountainside. It remains in view for a number of kilometres and becomes more and more spectacular the closer you get. This is the Viaduc du Caramel, which was part of a former tramway line between Menton and Sospel—an incredible and beautiful engineering feat.

You pass the village of Castillon with a few kilometres still to do; shortly after, the road forks with all motorised traffic that is heading to Sospel being taken through a tunnel, leaving the final stretch of road almost completely car-free, and there is no choice—bicycles aren't allowed in the tunnel. On that day, the tunnel was closed, and very little traffic came with us. The Col is marked by a roughly hewn and tiny tunnel of its own as you cross through one valley into another, leaving Menton and the coast behind you, and now with an amazing view of the Col de Braus to our left, the Turini, and the peaks of the Mercantour Park in front, and the Italian Alps to the right.

The southeastern ascent of the Col de Turini, our route starting in Sospel, is 24 kilometres, with an average gradient of 5% and a maximum gradient of 9%. It is known for its many lacets (hairpins) and scenic landscapes. I thought today's climbing was challenging in the heat but beautiful and worth it. Such great climbing. Kate may also have the same view, though she is known to spend quite some time digging in, with her head down, possibly with eyes closed, but looking at the road, or more likely, looking at her Garmin, a La Chris Froome. I'd like to think she's absorbed by the muscular, tanned Adonis in front of her…I never worked out how to finish this sentence without sobbing pitifully into the crook of my arm.

France, historically, is where edible snails come from, and the most sought-after wild snails, although they can be found around the world, are typically collected around the Alps. Having taken so long to arrive in the Alps (us, not the snails), I do feel that we are coming out of our shells.

Our accommodation for the night was delightful—a chalet-style hotel at the top of the mountain that was also a café/snack/bar—perfect. We had a lovely meal on its balcony, overlooking the Alps in the warm summer sun.

Day 48, 16th July, distance 43.53 kilometres (4,786.55 kilometres), elevation gain 971m (53,030m).

Depart: Col de Turini. Arrive: La Bolline.

Weather: 30 degrees, but it's a recovery day, so if we take it easy, it'll be fine.

Food: The usual, plus chicken/beef on a BBQ, melon, cured ham, cheese.

Having come out of our shells yesterday, it was a sluggish start today, though more down than up (just). Mercantour National Park is the area we are passing through, and it's an unbelievable place with regards to prehistory, flora, and fauna (and bees). There are times when you wonder if there are any humans living here. It's a protected national park with mountains, valleys, and villages. (Many of which are spectacularly perched, such as Belvedere, which we cycled by today.) There was only one climb today of the Col Saint-Martin, and that was less than 8 kilometres long if you exclude the now-anticipated 14-kilometre ride uphill to its base!

There are carvings on the rocks in some areas that date from Neolithic times. (Kate's mum and dad, Janet and Bernard, will no doubt recall them.) The area is popular with cyclists and walkers, with a diverse range of flora and fauna to be seen. The chamois have a large population here, so I made sure that mine was clean and well-buttered in case any tourists were hoping to catch a glimpse. Other wildlife to look for includes the marmot, ermine, ibex, red deer, hares, boar, and a range of birds of prey—that is some game pie. There are, apparently, also Italian wolves in the area, but I chose to put that out of my mind and didn't even mention it to Kate. Though I did have to stop myself from singing Van Morrison's 'Moondance', which was today's song in my head; it was used along with The Marcels' 'Blue Moon' (oh no, that's in my head now) in 'An American Werewolf in London'.

Our destination, La Bolline, is in the 'Val de Blore', a former glacial terrace that has formed into a shallow and pleasant valley planted with conifers and surrounded by mountains.

We spent an evening with Fred and Magda, (Magda is originally from Poland) and their two dogs. They have built themselves a home in La Bolline and offered very simple accommodation, with surprising comfort. It was a cheap stay, including breakfast, but they also provided food and drinks in the evening and spent time talking about their lives, how they live, and also showing an interest in our travels. The house had started out as a workshop, which Fred had reinforced and extended very simply.

As an example, the locks on the doors consisted of pieces of wood with a screw through the middle, allowing you to rotate the wooden 'catch' into a latch. It's difficult to describe this stay, but it is authentic, possibly unique, and a memorable experience. We didn't stay up late as we had a big ride the following day, so we took showers, then went to bed. The bedroom was small but practical, though not much bigger than the bed. I awoke in the night to see something I had never seen before, a glowworm or firefly hovering around the room, its patterns of light intermittently and hypnotically glowing, softly fading in and out. I wanted to watch it for longer, perhaps attempt to take a photo, but I drifted off into a restful sleep.

Day 49, 17th July, distance 89.33 kilometres (4,875.88 kilometres), elevation gain 2,238m (55,268m).

Depart: La Bolline. Arrive: Jausiers.

Weather: 30 degrees, but some blustery wind at the top, so be careful on the corners. Most of our days in the Alps start to cool in the shade of the valley and remain comfortable as we climb into cooler air higher up, which works well.

Food: Croissants, toast, chestnut spread, pain au chocolate, baguette, soup de poisson, white fish, vegetables.

When I first woke, I had forgotten it, but then remembered, "Did you see that glow worm last night?" I asked Kate.

"Yesss, wasn't it incredible? It was like turning on a Christmas light on a slow flash cycle, that was fantastic to see just floating around above us. I thought you were asleep."

"So did I."

Deep breath! Today we have the Col de la Bonnette—sometimes one climb is enough!

From the south, the climb starts at Saint-Etienne-de-Tinee and is 26 kilometres long. As with some of our other climbs, signs are placed every kilometre that provide information such as the distance to the summit and the average slope in the following kilometre. The average percentage is a steady 6.4% on the climb to the actual Col de la Bonette, but on the loop around the Cime de la Bonette, the gradient reaches at least 15%, and it feels exposed and a little scary! It had felt a little scary the previous few kilometres with the wind picking up. At one point, we emerged from a promontory, and the wind turned the tandem sideways across the road in one gust.

It happened in an instant, and though we were able to remain upright, we had to dismount and edge ourselves slowly around the corner. What is the loop? Basically, the pass is at 2,715 metres (The Col) but an extension, just a loop, was added in 1961 to celebrate my birth, and this takes the road up and 'round the peak, the Cime de la Bonette, reaching 2,802 metres and making it the highest through road in Europe, though arguably not a pass. Having already conquered the Cime when we did the Raid Alpine, we kept closer to the border with Italy today by turning at the Col which was also safer in the wind. Where did that come from, 'a promontory' it's a funny word and awkward to pronounce. I can't recall using the word before, yet I'm fairly sure it's the correct word to describe the rock formation. It makes you wonder what part of the brain that was stored in—I suppose somewhere just behind the nose.

Jausiers, our destination, is the start of the climb up the Col de la Bonette from the north, so basically the day was spent just cycling uphill and then down the other side, though to begin with that was very cautiously done until we were in lighter winds further down. Jausiers is also not very far from our next climb tomorrow. (Well, there's a surprise.) It was a nice, warm evening in Jausiers. The town seems to lie in the middle of a wide valley, and wherever you look, there are massive mountain ranges in every direction. We walked into town for a refreshing beer, but all the time we walked along, bumping into things whilst gazing around at the magnificent mountains. I imagine, though, that if you live here, you risk taking them for granite.

Day 50, 18th July, distance 43.69 kilometres (4,919.57 kilometres), elevation gain 955m (56,223m).

Depart: Jausiers Arrive: Guillestre.

Weather: 32 degrees. At one point, a rain cloud passed over and drenched the neighbouring mountain!

Food: Croissants, toast, fruit puree, yoghurt, cereal, baguette, banana, bread, camembert, pork, legumes.

Thankfully, it was only a short ride today—but of course, that still involves getting over a mountain that started just after 7 kilometres, where, on the grassy slopes, we were delighted to see some Marmottes out for silflay. It was nice and easy to begin with, "What's the average?" I hear you say, it's 5%, so that means some steep bits—up to 11% over about 15 kilometres in total. These short climbs are great! Life is great, and we are feeling great as we set off up the famous Col de Vars, only stopping to photograph the Marmottes. Are you ready for a wild ride from Jausiers to Guillestre? Buckle up your helmet and tighten up your cycle shoes, my friend, because we're in for some serious uphill battles and breathtaking downhill moments (don't tell Kate.)

"Was there something extra in your croissants this morning?" asked Kate.

As we start off in Jausiers, we're feeling pretty good about ourselves. The scenery is beautiful, the sun is shining, and our legs are feeling fresh. But let's be honest, this is just the calm before the storm.

Once you start climbing up the Col de Vars, you'll quickly realise that you're in for a real challenge. It's like climbing a never-ending staircase, except the stairs are steep and your legs are on fire. But fear not, my friend! As you approach the top, you'll be greeted with some stunning views of the surrounding mountains. (With a couple of kilometres to go, we heard some music coming up behind, and Kate seemed to have a surge of energy as the tandem accelerated. It turned out to be a cyclist who pushed the tandem from behind and kept going for 60–70 metres before saying 'Enjoy the rest of your trip' and taking off ahead of us.)

Take a moment to catch your breath and admire the scenery, because you're going to need it for the descent. As you start descending, you'll feel like you're flying down the mountain. The wind is in your hair, the sun is on your face, and your bike is swerving like a dolphin. It's exhilarating and terrifying all at the same time.

"Was it a couple of extra shots in your coffee?" asked Kate.

But don't get too cocky, because there are some hairpin turns that will have you questioning your life choices. You'll be screaming like a banshee as you navigate these curves, praying that you don't go flying off the edge of the mountain.

As you approach Guillestre, you'll feel like you've conquered the world. You've battled your way up the Col de Vars and survived the harrowing descent. You'll feel like a Tour de France champion, ready to take on any challenge that comes your way.

There you have it, a cycle over the Col de Vars from Jausiers to Guillestre. Just remember to enjoy the ride and don't take yourself too seriously. After all, it's just a bike ride! "Really?"

Guillestre is where we are staying, a beautiful village nestled amongst the mountains on the edge of the Queyras nature reserve between the passes of the Vars and the Izoard. The old ramparts of the town can be seen here, and there are old houses, narrow streets, and a gothic church. The church stands out, having a particularly tall bell tower. There's a not-to-be missed market with local produce on Monday mornings. It's Tuesday.

"Well, you came back down to earth with a bump." Kate said.

Our stay had a swimming pool, so for the second time this holiday, we went for a dip, and there are photos to prove it. ("No, that's okay, we believe you!") before enjoying a lovely meal in Guillestre.

It was a bit of a hiccup, but I don't recall having a serious talk about alcohol so far. It's unfortunate that we both like a drink, particularly a couple of large beers at the end of a ride. But in an attempt to manage our consumption and bring it to a healthier level, we have tried out a number of strategies during this tour. Initially we opted to only drink alcohol on weekends (Friday, Saturday, and Sunday), unless forced to break the rule for social reasons. But by midweek, it did seem like a long wait and risked us bingeing at the weekend. We then decided to change this to every other day.

That was a lot easier to cope with, until we got confused, like not knowing which day it was. We also couldn't remember whether we had drunk the day before or not (very convenient), which wasn't helped because every other day does mean, there weren't specific days of the week. Kate suggested that we only drink on days beginning with 'T', but that wasn't going to work. Tuesday, Thursday, today, and tomorrow. So finally, we moved to no-alcohol Mondays, Wednesdays, and Fridays. This has worked well, and we have continued with that pattern since finishing the tour. Changes (transitions between each routine) I'm embarrassed to say have always been 'in our favour' so that whilst changing from one approach to the new one, drinking was allowed leading up to starting the new pattern. (Mind you, we don't go mad, usually just a pint or two…occasionally with a digestif 'pousse-café' for medicinal purposes!)

Day 51, 19th July, distance 51.32 kilometres (4,970.89 kilometres), elevation gain 1,448m (57, 671m).

Depart: Guillestre. Arrive: Briancon.

Weather: 32 degrees, again more pleasant over the climb.

Food: Croissants, baguettes, yoghurt, fruit, bread, eggs, ham, game pie, salad, truffle linguine.

'A new version of hell', not the linguine, Jacques Goddet's opinion of the terrain around the Col d'Izoard, and he was director of the Tour de France (1936–1986).

The Col d'Izoard is about 16 kilometres from the southern direction and has an average of 7.5% with a maximum 10% or so I convinced myself. In fact, it turns out that the climbing starts at our doorstep in Guillestre, meaning that we are about 32 kilometres uphill. This does bring the average gradient down to under 5% because, thankfully, the first 16 kilometres are gradual until you get to those 16 kilometres to go. But flat or downhill to that 16-kilometre mark would still have been less daunting. Still, only one climbed again today and then downhill to Briancon. So, where does the climb officially start? I checked this, and Wikipedia says that it starts at Guillestre and is 31.5 kilometres. But they go on to say that the climb 'proper' starts near Chateau Queyras, where the ascent is 15.9 kilometres. It's this next section, though, that takes you through the distinctive Casse-Deserte with its barren screes punctured by giant thorns of huge rock pillars. They appear to be everywhere, and they are both beautiful and eerie. There is little vegetation about it, but it is home to Marmottes. (Not all of them, evidently, unless they travel a long way for their breakfast.)

It puts things in context when you cycle down a mountain and the place you stay is a city that is still at an altitude of over 1,325 metres, the highest city in France. The city regularly features in the Tour de France and is therefore a popular place for cyclists. We had an excellent meal in Briancon. My starter was pate en croute which looked like an amazing slice of game pie (I made the right choice!) and truffle linguine, which didn't look amazing but was. Kate had something else; she said, "This is something else."

<u>Day 52</u>, 20th July, distance 70.43 kilometres (5,041.32 kilometres) elevation gain 1,540m (59,211m).

Depart: Briancon. Arrive: Saint Michel de Maurienne.

Weather: 28 degrees, comfortable; couldn't ask for more.

Food: Pain au chocolate; yoghurt, fruit puree; apricots, cereal, doughnuts, baguettes, mackerel, goat's cheese salad, steak, sweet potato frites, and salad.

Today it's only one climb away, but the way my brain works, you get Lauteret, Galibier, and Telegraphe included. Well, that's what I had thought! The Lauteret was a fast, easy, and thoroughly enjoyable 26 kilometres, but then the 8 kilometres plus up the Galibier were further and somewhat more challenging than I had realised. Admittedly, most cyclists would say that it's just the Lauteret and the Galibier in this direction. The Lauteret road is fairly busy (quiet compared to the UK), at least compared to most climbs that we have done. But it's worth it for the great views of glaciers that still ice the cake, the Massif des Ecrins, and the views down the valleys.

It's also not too steep if you don't include the extra few kilometres to carry on up to the Galibier. How lucky we were when we got to the turn-off for the Galibier, and it was a reserve morning for cyclists only. Wonderful. We really loved today's climbs and found ourselves putting in rather more effort than is necessary just to complete a tour! It's an absolutely magical climb. Approaching the summit of the Galibier, there's a memorial to the founder of the Tour de France, Henri Desgrange, who once wrote about the Galibier, "In front of this giant we can do nothing but take our hats off and bow," he obviously didn't desperately need the toilet.

The descent down the Galibier is steep and quite challenging for a tandem with touring gear on, and it's about 18 kilometres to Valloire. But after the gentle 4 kilometres up to the Col de Telegraphe for the bonus Col, it's then a lovely, wide, and sweeping descent to our destination.

Saint Michel de Maurienne is probably the type of place that you pass through. It's about 700 metres above sea level, which is quite high. But as we'll see, there's still a long way to go to our next climb! When you look at places to visit, other than an aluminium museum (and I don't mean a museum made from aluminium), most places to visit are within a 20-kilometre radius, rather than in town. I think I could work in a museum like that, "Excuse me sir, what is this?"

"It's aluminium."

"And that, over there?"

"Let me just check. Yes, a bit of a surprise one that, it's more aluminium."

There is a very sad story about the town, though. On 12 December 1917, there was a railway accident involving a troop train carrying French soldiers home for leave from the Italian Front in the Great War. (Which, in fact, it wasn't 'great', that is.) As the train descended on the Maurienne Valley, it derailed, causing a catastrophic crash and subsequent fire in which more than 675 died. An unbelievable loss of life in tragic times. In the evening, Kate and I were able to locate a memorial to the victims of the accident, and, as often with these incidents, there is much more to the story. The accident was censored by the military, perhaps to not demoralise people at this point in the war but perhaps to conveniently cover up criminal negligence. A number of human errors were made:

Due to a local shortage of engines, the commanding officer directed 19 coaches to be coupled with one engine. (There would usually be two engines, but one was requisitioned for a munitions train.)

Only three coaches had compressed-air brakes; the rest either had none or had hand brakes that required guards to operate.

It is believed that the train was also overloaded for operation on a downhill rail track. (Modane to Saint Michel de Maurienne averages over 3% downhill.)

The driver objected to taking the train on safety grounds but was threatened with court martial by his superior. The driver tried to manage the situation by driving very slowly from the start of the journey, but ultimately, the engine and the brakes available were not enough to manage the weight and momentum of the full train. Its speed gradually increased and became out of control, and ultimately it derailed. Fire ripped through the carriages, and many victims could not be identified. The reporting was significantly suppressed by the military; it's believed that over 800 soldiers lost their lives.

A memorial was inaugurated at the crash site near La Saussaz, just outside St Michel, that Kate and I walked to. It's believed to be the worst rail disaster in history, due to an operational error.

Day 53, 21st July, distance 60.38 kilometres, (5,101.70 kilometres), elevation gain 1,290m (60,501m).

Depart: Saint Michel de Maurienne. Arrive: Bonneval-Sur-Arc.

Weather: Sunny spells, 28 degrees, very pleasant.

Food: Croissants, cereal, yoghurt, baguette, salmon pate, egg, banana, pain au raisins, deliciously juicy burger, frite, salad.

The route today is uphill all day, and we don't even get to tick off a Col!

We remain close to Italy; passing the border town of Modane, you can walk over the high mountains or take the Fréjus road and rail tunnel (unless you're on a bike) into Italy. Its buildings are painted in bright colours and have wrought iron balconies that are reminiscent of parts of Italy. Located 1000 metres above sea level, Modane is also a mountain town, which puts tomorrow's climb in context as we continue up well above 2,000 metres heading into Vanoise National Park.

We passed the Marie-Therese Redoubt, a massive, fortified complex built by the Kingdom of Sardinia at the start of the 19th century. It is just one of five forts that make up the Esseillon barrier. The forts were designed to block the enemy's path (the French). Ultimately, they served no purpose following the re-annexation of the Savoy to France in 1860, with France gaining a money-making future tourist destination in the process.

By the time we reached Bonneval-sur-Arc, our overnight stop, we had climbed to about 1800m, higher than most cycling passes in France. There must be a pass or a Col in there somewhere. It'll be a short climb tomorrow. (No, it won't, John.)

Subsequently, I did find a Col that we had passed through on today's route. The Col de La Madeleine, amongst other races, featured in stage 19 of the 2019 Tour de France. Starting in Lanslevillard, it's only 4.2 kilometres, but with an average gradient of 6.7% and a maximum of 10%, it doesn't go unnoticed and is a nice, winding climb. In fact, I revisited the day's profile, and the climb sticks out like a Col that is sticking up out of the profile, of a long, gradual climb, can't be missed! This stage had no winner as it was neutralised due to landslides up ahead on the Col de L'Iseran! I recall watching this on television and seeing mud sliding across the road in front of a team car. Although there were no stage winners, times were taken according to position at the time, which meant that Egan Bernal moved into the yellow jersey on the day and went on to become the first Columbian to win the tour.

Cycling on the D902 beside the Arc River, you eventually end up at Bonneval-sur-Arc and either stop or go over the highest pass in Europe, the Col de L'Iseran. It's a pretty little village, and though small, we found a nice bar to eat in, which we really needed.

Day 54, 22nd July, distance 60.40 kilometres (5,162.10 kilometres) elevation gain 1059m (61,560m).

Depart: Bonneval-Sur-Arc Arrive: Bourg-Saint-Maurice.

Weather: 8 degrees at Bonneval and even cooler on top! But 28 degrees in Bourg!

Food: Cereal bars, apricots, fruit puree, cereal biscuits, peanuts, salad, moussaka.

The Col de L'Iseran climb starts in Bonneval at the bottom of our road. Who needs a warm-up anyway? It's almost 13 kilometres short (from this side!), averages 7% with a maximum of 11%, and the pass is at 2763m above sea level. Wow, it felt like the top last night!

The Col de L'Iseran is fantastic and almost out of this world, literally. We are slow straight away, which always means it's steep. It's a long, slow drag, but there's no panic; we've got a lot of downhill to come, and there is no rush. There was respite where the terrain was fairly flat, possibly for 1 kilometre maybe just under, but only for it to get even steeper to keep up the average! It's a little unworldly—very little vegetation and seems to get steeper and slower. We are so glad this is the only climb today. But at the top, though cold, the weather is clear, and we quickly get on with the scary descent. (I would cope better if it was in a cloud, and I couldn't see the scary drops at the side of the road.)

The previous time we cycled up the Iseran, it was in the opposite direction, and I recall staying in Val d'Isere the night before. I also recall the name from the 1992 Winter Olympics. But we are headed for the Alpine town of Bourg-Saint-Maurice—the gateway to the Tarentaise Valley, which makes it an ideal base for exploring the valley's famous ski resorts and great for walking and mountain biking in the summer. It is also known for a KV (Vertical Kilometre) cycling event held annually. It's the start of the 48-kilometre climb up the Col from the other side!

This sounds great—a long, steady downhill—but I had a good look and could not find a practical alternative; the road between Val d'Isere and Tignes has numerous (7 or 8) dark tunnels, and the sound of traffic is shocking. Bike lights are essential (I brought a second rear and front light specifically for these tunnels.) and at least this time it's flat or downhill, so quicker to get through and more able to keep up with the traffic. On that day, though, they were not bad at all, quite enjoyable, and plenty of other cyclists passed. It was a very fast descent to Bourg, with most traffic going in the opposite direction. It couldn't have been bad because Kate enjoyed it! I wouldn't say it was something to avoid.

At Bourg, we are still on the Italian border and still high in the mountains. Bourg has access to one of the largest ski resorts there, known as the Paradiski, and has direct rail routes to London and Amsterdam. We were amazed at the Arc en Ciel funicular railway that goes from the town to the Arc 100 ski area. The trains are very modern and futuristic and have large panoramic windows. It is electric, and it climbs 810 metres in under 3 kilometres with a maximum gradient of 39%, making it efficient and spectacular.

Day 55, 23rd July, distance 84.44 kilometres (5,246.54 kilometres), elevation gain 2409m (63.969m).

Depart: Bourg-Saint-Maurice Arrive: Demi-Quartier.

Weather: 28 degrees, sunny spells.

Food: cereals, yoghurt, apple puree, croissants, baguettes, eggs, mackerel pate, gum sweets, plum tomatoes, carrots, radishes, tuna pasta salad, peanuts.

We now have the Cormet de Roseland; blimey, every day is epic. Starting from our doorstep, yet again we headed north from Bourg-Saint-Maurice to tackle the 19 kilometres that lie ahead. We had been up the Cormet de Roseland before, but from the opposite direction and via the beautiful Col de Pres, and my recollection of the descent (today's climb) was that it was stunning, with plenty of bends and Alpine meadows. I also recall seeing the Lac de Roseland and its stunning azure colour, and I was looking forward to that view again. Azure? One of those words that is in my brain somewhere, and when I manage to locate it, "Wow, just the word I needed to find the perfect description," even if I shouldn't have been so self-azure. Roseland is more of an emerald colour!

We immediately met that forever-present 7% gradient. It's not that hard that we won't survive, but, especially with panniers on, it's hard enough to feel like we're wading into snail mucus. I can remember statistics that said the average was a much more forgiving 5%, but only a couple of kilometres in, and we got a downhill section. That explains it, and very soon we are back into the 7% plus stuff for a few kilometres, and it's all fairly straight. Then we got there—the zigzag bit that I recalled. It's wonderful, and Kate and I can never get enough of it. I must think about why that is. Hairpins—nine of them, one after another. They don't last long, but the climb seems to have gone on forever (in a nice way) and we are only about halfway.

Now for the Col des Saises. We have been and continue to be spoilt by the climbs we have done and will continue to do on this journey. Having descended from the Cormet de Roseland, we cycled through Beaufort and ahead had 15 kilometres of climbing, in and out through forests, and averaging 7% finishing in the town of Les Saisies. Like me, to my wife, town finishes are always a bit of a disappointment. In fairness, it's a nice Alpine town and is on the 'Route des Grande Alpes', a tourist route that starts at Lac Leman and travels over the Alps to the French Riviera. (Or, in reverse, basically our route for the last week!) We have seen signposts indicating that we have regularly been on the route on our journey.

Demi-Quartier wasn't a destination that I had high hopes for. Nonetheless, as you approach Demi-Quartier, you're struck by the serene and picturesque beauty of this charming location. The first thing you notice is the fresh mountain air and the breathtaking views of the snow-capped peaks of the French Alps—and there, towering above the opposite side of the valley, is Mont Blanc! Stunning, clear, snow-covered and immense, it is the highest mountain peak in Europe. The stunning beauty of the mountain range and the peaceful atmosphere of the village make for a truly unforgettable experience, other than the lack of a nearby restaurant, so a healthy shop bought tea for us. Our accommodation is superbly positioned to face across the valley and watch Mont Blanc, the cloud formations, and the changing views, and we are both in awe of the view. I think we earnt it!

There is a sense that we are coming to the last part of our trip, with a couple of rest days coming up, followed by one big climb, and then the Alps are almost complete, and we have covered well over 5,000 kilometres. The bike is performing well, and we remain fit and healthy. It will have been about 4 weeks since our last rest day, and that stretch was always a slight concern for me, but the 'recovery' rides seem to have successfully seen us through. I say to Kate, "We still have a lot to do, though, we have a long way to go. Things can still go wrong, and we need to continue to do what we have been doing." "I know, but what we have done is already amazing."

Day 56, 25th July, distance 49.53 kilometres (5,296.07 kilometres), elevation 642m (64,611m).

Depart: Demi-Quartier. Arrive: Samoens.

Weather: Thunderstorms, 15 degrees, rain, occasional sunny spell 19 degrees.

Food: Brioche, yoghurt, cereal biscuit, pain au raisin, charcuterie, Papet Savoyard.

Today is a transition day to get us to Samoens for a couple of days of R&R with just 50 kilometres of cycling. Having said that, about halfway, we take a right turn at a small village called Balme and head upwards as though taking the direct route over the ski resorts to Samoens. At this point, thunder is rumbling around the mountains above, and we have to make a quick stop to put our rain jackets on. We do have a not-insignificant climb, the Colline d'Escargot to Araches-La-Frasse (about 7 kilometres), curving pleasantly up to the town under cliff faces and through wooded cliffs on the route to Flaine, but then the route curves back around and down to Chatillon-Sur-Cluses before circling 'round the mountain range to Samoens at a fast pace.

Although the Raid Alpine misses Samoens, for our trip, it was necessary to pass this way as it's nearer to the border with Switzerland. (We are past Italy now.) But we also wanted to visit this traditional mountain town, as we had stayed here as a base for skiing. (When I had an accident and a multiple fracture of my right ankle.) The slopes directly above Samoens are numerous and perfect for beginners and very experienced skiers. The resort also benefits from ski slopes and lifts that link with Morillon down the road and over the mountain to Les Carroz and Flaine. We liked it and thought it would be a great base for cycling during the summer months. Having a couple of rest days here, we hoped, would be a nice reward for getting this far and a different type of break from our last visit.

Samoens might be a modern, up-to-date ski resort, but it was once a mediaeval town. A thriving mediaeval centre for stone masons, it is now a charming mountain town that relies mostly on tourism as its number one income provider, even in the summer months, with ski shops switching their trade to cycling and walking. The centre is pedestrianised with attractive streets, colourful shops, and enticing bars and restaurants. We went to a bar and joined in with a pub quiz when we were skiing. I recall the team (of strangers) turning to me when a Tour de France question came up!

"How many stages are there in the Tour de France." I did one of those things when you overthink the question, "is it a trick question? It can depend, always 20 stages with an addition of a prologue." Wrong, it's 21. I recall the team of strangers turning to stare at me as one. A similar thing has happened to me since I was left in a room with 3 scary dogs, and they were play-fighting. I said, "Stop!"

Which they did immediately, and in unison, they turned and stared at me, a fresh steak sitting on a sofa.

The town has an impressive and substantial 8-person gondola, which means that the Grand Massif is accessible from the edge of the town. How many people can it carry? "Is it a trick question? It can depend; do two small children count as one?"

In Samoens, we were enjoying a beer in a bar when we arrived in the early afternoon, and we struck up a conversation with a couple on the table next to us. They were fascinated by our tour and thought it was an impressive feat, but we were equally astounded by theirs. They were in the process of walking across the French Alps carrying their camping gear on their backs. (Although that night they were having a 'recovery' by staying in a hotel.) This couple were each 75 years old! The man was very excited about our tandem (he had previously enjoyed cycling) but his partner had no interest, so he promptly took her over to show her the tandem—he was evidently still working on it.

Before going out in the evening, there was an electrical storm with rain absolutely pelting down. The view from our room went from mountains and meadows to a curtain of rain that hid the neighbourhood. We were temporarily lucky; however, the rain paused and, though water left the roads looking like rivers, we were able to go out to enjoy some traditional local food. Favourite meals include Fondue Savoyarde, Raclette cheese, and La Tartiflette, a dish made with gratinated potatoes, white wine, Reblochon cheese, onions, and smoked salted pork. My choice was similar to this, called Papet Savoyard, and had a variety of local sausages on top instead of cheese and leaks, rather than onions. It was delicious. A Facebook follower, Michael Foos, was so taken by my photo of it that he requested the ingredients so he could attempt to make it himself. (I'm easily impressed.) My other highlight was a dessert that I had, crème brûlée with Genepi. It was amazing. Crème Brûlée went from enjoyable to orgasmic. Genepi is a traditional herbal liqueur from the Alps. Genepi also refers to the Alpine plant commonly called wormwood and it is that which provides the flavour and colour. It is related to absinthe, though the devil is in the details of production, of course. The devil is definitely in there somewhere!

By the way, you probably haven't forgotten about my 'temporarily lucky' comment about the rain pausing. Our return to the chalet after our meal involved tiptoeing around puddles, dashing from doorway to doorway, and edging under canopies and balconies to attempt to keep dry—the torrential rain had returned.

Mind you, the excellent meal, along with the alcohol, meant that we found it funnier than anything and arrived back feeling and looking like happy but not quite drowned rats!

In the centre of town, an ornate gate marks the entrance to the Samoens botanical gardens. They are well worth a visit, and with free entry, you may as well! They are an opportunity to look at a large collection of Alpine flora and fauna on the hill overlooking the town. This does provide great views of the town up a steep, zigzagging pathway, if you have the energy.

Whilst in Samoens, we also had time to walk alongside the river Giffre to the Gorges de Tines. Over thousands of years, the river has dug through limestone rocks, forming a spectacular gorge with vertical cliffs probably 30 to 40 metres deep. The river gouged an earlier gorge, which I believe can be climbed through, before altering its course to create a second gorge. The route currently taken by a Giffre is very narrow, only 2 m wide in places. It is popular for white water rafting and canyoning. Having walked to the gorge without being rained on again, our intention was to catch the free 'ski' bus back to town, but a French couple offered us a lift just as the torrential rain retuned.

"That is kind of you, but we are okay, thank you." Kate said.

Luckily, they paused and allowed me to say, "Wait a minute, of course we would love a lift!" We would have been drenched, and driving back into town, you could hardly see where you were going because of the rain!

That evening, we enjoyed another lovely meal, and I was able to try the more well-known tartiflette. I reluctantly avoided the crème brûlée, though, in order to enjoy an espresso and grappa. (Well, we were not far from Italy!) Grappa is a grape-based Italian pomace brandy made by distilling the skins, pulp, seeds, and stems (i.e., the pomace) left over from winemaking. Grappa is primarily served as a digestif. (Its main purpose is to aid in the digestion of heavy meals, like that was ever proven, but I love the argument.) Grappa may be added to espresso coffee to create a caffè corretto, or a variation of this is the ammazzacaffè when the espresso is drunk first, followed by a few ounces of grappa served in its own glass. In Veneto, there is resentin; after finishing a cup of espresso with sugar, a few drops of grappa are poured into the nearly empty cup, swirled, and drunk down in one sip. I chose to go for a separate glass of grappa but added a little to my espresso dregs to finish it off. Very nice, slept well, no indigestion.

Day 57, 27th July, distance 58.66 kilometres (5,354.73 kilometres), elevation gain 1,852m (66,463m).

Depart: Samoens. Arrive: Bas Thex.

Weather: Clouds clearing to leave a hot, sunny day, 29 degrees.

Food: Croissants, baguettes, apricot, jam, cereal bars, fruit puree, cereal biscuit, Tartichevre, (I'm on a roll) baguette, olives, yoghurt. (Fortunately, I don't suffer from indigestion.)

At breakfast, whilst talking to a French couple and the host, we explained our route and also mentioned the difficult 'unknown' climb that we had had to tackle when we had first turned into the Pyrenees some time ago. The husband, Philippe, explained, "It's like alcohol; if it has no name, it's more dangerous."

When we came here to ski, and fantastic skiing it is (in my vastly experienced knowledge totalling 9 days of skiing), I thought what a great place this would be to cycle, as I looked across the valley from our accommodation to the Grand Massif. Little did I know at the time that just behind me was a significant Tour de France Climb, the Col de Joux Plane.

What the bloody hell was that all about? Did we rest for too long? Was it because the climb started immediately from Samoëns? Was it because we thought, that's it, Alps finished, job done? Whatever it was, this crept up on us. The Col de la Joux Plane is just one hard slug—sorry, slog. I had to check the stats afterwards; gradient was between 8–11%. So that'll be 9.5% then, for 11.8 kilometres!

We got a false sense of security coming out of Samoens. Pleased to be back on the bike, it is pleasant enough to spin your legs for a couple of hundred metres until you get to a switchback. Forget that; it's tough from now on and disorientating! The switchbacks keep coming, but sometimes going east then west, sometimes north then south—you have no idea where the road is going. At this point, I had to stop writing as I had a dizzy spell, honestly, and that sort of pre-migraine eye-blur. This road isn't carving its way where the road builders chose to go; it's just following the 'easiest' route up and over. This really is a tough climb—with quite a long 13% at one point—and some of it is unrelenting. But tip: just lift your head up and look around: pine-scented forests, spectacular views, smooth curving roads, wood-built chalets, and glimpses of Mont Blanc like you'll never see. In fact, it was a really great climb.

Avoriaz next, a bit like xylophone, you don't pronounce the z. After about 23 kilometres, you arrive in Morzine. (The downhill from the Col felt similar to the uphill and equally disorientating. Take care if you are on a tandem as the turns are tight, the type where you are gripping your brake leavers 'round corners and uncleating your foot to hang it out and help with balance.) Straight on, and it's only a little over 30 kilometres to the finish today, but not for us. We turned right and added on a 25-kilometre loop that took in the 14-kilometre climb up to Avoriaz (average 6%, maximum 11%.) The climb starts gently out of Morzine before hitting some switchbacks at about 3 kilometres and the joys of 9 to 11%.

But by about halfway, the gradient eases as you see the futuristic looking buildings of Avoriaz up in the distance before kicking up to around 7% again at some point. With just over 1 kilometre to go, we had to pass our left turn in order to complete the climb, passing a café, would you believe? This definitely was not in line with my rules for the tour. (Other than the one about doing whatever we want.) However, across a roundabout, then 100m or so to the finish in the resort, and then a U-turn to head back to the café for lunch, was worthwhile. We had a good break here, a meal, and a rest before taking the turn down the mountain. We were in for incredible views all around, and lots of mountain bikers zoomed off down tracks after having taken the cable lifts up. Then past a lake full of people enjoying a sunny day in or on the Lac de Montriond.

Our destination, Bas Thex, is just past Saint-Jean-d'Aulps. Let's just think about where we are, between Lake Geneva and Mont Blanc, and at the foot of the Roc d'Enfer mountain!

In winter, this must be a charming village-resort surrounded by fir trees and dressed in snow. Apparently, there's a 20-kilometre forest ski circuit, allowing you to slalom between the trees or splat into them like a poorly aimed snowball.

In the summer, though, this is a place for walking and cycling. In the Saint-Jean-d'Aulps, resort, the cable car takes lazy walkers and mountain bikers to 1500 metres, where they can make the most of routes amid the foothills of the Alps. Between Le Bas Thex and d'Aulps there is an 11th-century Cistercian abbey, the Abbaye d'Aulps. Abbaye was founded at the end of the 11th century. The monks who lived here were encouraged to join the Cistercian order in 1136, and before long, the Abbaye became one of the most powerful monasteries in mediaeval Savoie. The church was largely destroyed in 1823, was then largely overlooked or forgotten, and by 1998, the grounds were used mainly for farming. There is now a visitors' centre, and part of the Abbaye has been renovated, giving an insight into the daily routine of the monks that lived there in the Middle Ages.

One thing you do discover, cycling around France are the strangest names for places that often do not even sound like or look French to me. We were in Bas Thex tonight, what? Well, I could find no information about what, after all, is just a hamlet. My guess is the base of the Thex. I didn't find the Thex, so I couldn't be sure, but we were scarily close to the base of a massive rock face!

Day 58, 28th July, distance 88.18 kilometres (5,442.91 kilometres), elevation gain 1,117m (67, 580m).

Depart: Bas Thex. Arrive: Veigy-Foncenex.

Weather: Sunny spells, 28 degrees, occasionally a strong headwind!

Food: Croissants, baguettes, rusks, crab paste, mentos, apple puree, peanuts, bruschetta, and Napoletana pizza.

Down to Lac Leman today, well, apart from Col de Corbier. It's possibly the last climb in the Northern Alps before you hit the lake. It's a bit steep, but only a few kilometres to the top. As is our habit, we preview our route and any climbs the evening before to plan the next day. Unfortunately, on this occasion, after an internet search, I pulled up the wrong profile for the climb and we did not think it deserved much consideration, so we were a little shocked to find that this was a tough climb, and very tough for the last 4 kilometres. It felt good though to still have such good riding here with an average of 8 % and a maximum of 11%, there were ominous dark clouds all around, though escaping the mountains ultimately meant escaping the rain.

When we first spotted Lac Leman, it was just an occasional glimpse into the distance, but soon it appeared to be within reach as we continued downhill. We were getting hungry and decided it would be nice to stop for a picnic beside the lake. That was a bit of a mistake. The distance to the lake was very deceptive, it seemed to be within reach for about an hour before we finished our descent. With that empty pit feeling in your stomach, we needed the place we found to stop. It was a nice park beside the lake, though, and we knew it would be almost flat for the rest of the day.

Evian-Les-Bains, or just Evian, is of course known for its mineral water, which is exported internationally. Beside the lake and close to the Alps, it is a popular tourist destination. Evian was featured in the Tour de France in 1925, and the following year was used for the 'Grand Depart', (the start) the first time it had started outside of Paris (though this is the norm these days.) This was the longest edition of Le Tour, 5745 kilometres. The winner, the Belgian Lucien Buysse, was, on stage three, advised that his daughter had died and only continued to compete after being persuaded to do so by his family. The Tour de France win by Lucien Buysse in 1926 was special for several reasons.

Firstly, Buysse was not considered a top contender for the race, as he was relatively unknown and had never won a major race before. He was also riding for a relatively unknown team, Alcyon.

Secondly, Buysse's victory was significant because he was the first Belgian to win the Tour de France. This was a major achievement for Belgian cycling, and Buysse's win helped to establish Belgium as a major force in the sport.

Finally, Buysse's victory was notable for the way he won the race. He was in third place going into the final stage, which was a ridiculous 342-kilometre ride from Metz to Dunkerque. Buysse was able to break away from the other riders and ride solo for most of the stage, winning it and, by doing so, securing an overall victory. Buysse's win is still celebrated in Belgium today, and he is remembered as one of the country's greatest cyclists. (They have a few!)

We passed through Thonon-Les-Bains, the starting point for the Raid Alpine, on the way to Veigy-Foncenex, which feels like a strange place to arrive tucked in a corner near Lac Leman—we can't go any further without crossing the border into Switzerland (Geneva) and tomorrow we'll be skirting around the edge into the Jura mountains (the Jura what?). Today and tomorrow we were viewed as 'transition days' and we just needed to get on with it and then move on, but in fact both involved some lovely cycling.

Day 59, 29th July, distance 85.64 kilometres (5,528.55 kilometres), elevation gain 900m (68,480m).

Depart: Veigy-Foncenex. Arrive: Gex.

Weather: Overcast, a few light showers, 23 degrees. We can't really complain; it has been nice throughout the Alps.

Food: Pain au chocolate, chèvre yoghurt, pureed apple, banana, biscottes, sardines, strawberry tart, charcuterie, lasagne, peanuts.

We crossed the Rhone today as it flows from Lac Leman on its journey to eventually spill into the Mediterranean, where we last crossed it on day 42 by ferry. The Rhône is a significant river in France (and Switzerland), rising in the Alps and flowing west and south through Lac Leman and southeastern France before discharging into the Mediterranean Sea.

The Jura Mountain range is a short distance north of the Western Alps and demarcates a significant portion of the French-Swiss border. While the Jura range proper is located in France and Switzerland, the range continues northeastwards through northern Switzerland and Germany. I can tell you, there has been no expense and no stone turned in to providing you with the information in this book!

Not long before the end of our ride today, I catch a glimpse of futuristic buildings reminiscent of Futuroscope, a theme park in the south-west of France, but by the time I look back to complete the last few kilometres of our ride, I have forgotten about them.

We stayed in Gex, just a few kilometres from the border with Switzerland and 15 kilometres from Geneva, but other than a pleasant hotel and a nice pizza, it's the sort of place that is hard to recall. We evidently did not have the time to look around. Gex 'to be' was inhabited around 1800 BC, and around 220 BC, the Gaesatae, a group of Gallic warriors, were living in the area, after which the town was part of Roman Gaul. Since then, it has at various times been under the jurisdiction of France, Switzerland, and the Duchy of Savoie. There is evidently quite a lot of history in the place, but we didn't find the time to dig a little.

Day 60, 30th July, distance 99.44 kilometres (5,627.99 kilometres), elevation gain 1,508m (69,988m).

Depart: Gex. Arrive: Pontarlier.

Weather: 18 degrees, 6 degrees in the clouds, bitterly cold downhill.

Food: Absinthe.

Tour de France Climb—The Col de la Faucille!

"How much I had heard of that pass! How steep it was to be, and how terrible the three kilometres to the top! To mount them, I ate two breakfasts, one after the other." (E. Pennell, Over the Alps on a Bicycle.) This isn't France as I know it. It has begun to have a very different feel. But this is a beautiful climb, and when you are not amongst trees, there are amazing views, taking in Geneva, Mont Blanc, Lac Leman, and another glimpse of those futuristic buildings. What are they? Whilst we stop to take in the view (and shelter from a shower), I do a quick search on my phone—it's CERN, the European organisation for nuclear research—think particle acceleration, and very recently, they confirmed (as Einstein predicted) that dark matter does fall with gravity. Are we standing over the tunnel? Is it safe?

The weather, at this point, was a bit disappointing. We had started in sunshine, but from about halfway up the climb, it just got wetter and colder. You wouldn't know that we are basically fair-weather cyclists, mainly training in a bike-hut at home on our Wattbikes and using Zwift. But on a tour, you get on with it—and cycling is always good. (Except when it isn't.) The Col is 1,323 metres, and you suddenly realise that you really are back in the mountains again. The route, almost along the top of the mountain range, also meant that we were only gradually dropping the height we had gained today, cycling mainly in cold, damp conditions, until we got to the Cote des Rousses after about 12 kilometres, still at 1,097 metres and desperate for some warmth and hot chocolate.

Stops like this rarely warm you up thoroughly enough, though, because you are chilled to the bone. Then it was time for the real downhill, which plummeted down to Morez. It would have been great in the sun, but no, we got even colder, so very soon you could feel the tandem shaking with cold beneath us. This was a 7-kilometre downhill run very close to the border with Switzerland, leading us to another climb from Morez to the Lac de Bellefontaine. We got to the bottom expecting to stop again, but suddenly the sun shone gloriously, so we kept cycling to help the warmth spread through the muscles to the bones. It's quite a slow process, but after about three-quarters of an hour, we were feeling great again as we pressed on up this 11-kilometre climb. It was very pleasant, averaging 3.6% with an insignificant maximum approaching 9%. (Flat is beginning to be the only insignificant incline, to be honest. I think I may become a flat earth advocate; it seems like it could be a simpler, easier outlook to deny the existence of science.)

Today was quite a long day in the saddle, which is always fascinating when you look back on these days and can't believe the amount you have done and seen. After the climb, we found ourselves gliding along long, straight, shallow valleys with beautiful meadows and farmsteads, lined with pine forests. The buildings are unfamiliar, with nearly every house, farm, and even churches, having a tin roof with a metal facia, often ornately decorated, on the south-facing wall. A Facebook follower, Ugluk Urukai (it seems I am followed by Orcs) explained that it's for the snow.

When we stopped for a bite to eat in a small village, we could see a structure dominating the skyline above the pine trees. It was difficult to decide if this was a natural feature or, because it was so regular and shear, whether it was man-made, but we were fascinated by it. Ugluk came to the rescue again with "La Roche Champion à Chapelle des Bois." The Champion Rock in Chapelle des Bois (I fear I'm being hunted; he's tricking and tracking us). A local walk appeared to take in the natural features of the Swiss border along the source of the Doubs, a river that was to become a fellow traveller for a day or two.

Shortly before reaching Pontarlier, to our right was a pass, the Cluse de Pontarlier, a gateway between La Cluse and Pontarlier that seemed to be heavily guarded by two castles facing each other from each side of the pass. Ugluk Urukai appeared from nowhere to explain that what we could see was the Chateau de Joux on the left and Fort Mahler on the right. It appeared he had us trapped. Fortune favours the brave, however, and our road swept around to the left, keeping clear of the castles and the narrow entrance into the pass. In any case, it transpired that Ugluk had miscalculated our direction of escape and the Uruk-hai were on the other side of the valley. (So, Chateau de Joux was on the right and Fort Mahler on the left—Ugluk admitted to his error.)

Chateau de Joux is evidently in a strategic position above the Cluse Pass and has been an important military location for centuries. An early chateau, was built by the Joux family in the Middle Ages, and this was purchased by Philip the Good (I sense irony in the name), the powerful Duke of Burgundy. Since then, Joux has been regularly enlarged and fortified as it has passed through the ownership of many over the years.

On the opposite side of the pass, Fort Mahler (originally, Fort du Larmont Inferieure) was built between 1843 and 1851 to cover the side of the Chateau de Joux from possible attack. (Previously, the Austrians and the Swiss had both successfully attacked the Joux from this side, so further defence from the darker forces of Mordor was needed.)

So, we are still in a mountain range, and I am surprised. I knew little about the Jura and certainly did not realise that it ran close to the border. Pontarlier is at an altitude of 837 m and in the heart of the Jura Mountains. Pontarlier was very well known due to the production of absinthe at the beginning of the last century (Why am I minded spelling it with a 'y', Absynthe?). Today, the city has not one but two distilleries producing absinthe again. Or is it just one? I'm fairly sure I saw two, and they were spinning.

Wormwood (once scrubbed) is the primary ingredient that gives absinthe its unmistakable botanical bitterness and has been associated with mythical beings and magical connotations since ancient times. Absinthe also has particular status as one of the only spirits to have been specifically banned by governments in the early 1900s. (Bad news is good news for business, better than no news, of course!)

But drinkable wormwood goes back much further, with mentions in ancient Egyptian and Syrian texts as well as the Bible. It was used to treat ailments such as jaundice, anaemia, and bad breath for much longer than an alcoholic beverage. It wasn't until the late 1700s that absinthe in its current form was developed in Switzerland, resulting in headaches, liver failure, and bad breath. However, its dubious reputation as a medicine remained, and it was given to French soldiers during their colonial conquest of Algeria as a fever and malaria preventative. Perhaps unsurprisingly, by the time soldiers returned to France, they had developed a taste for absinthe, and it quickly became a popular drink with a mythical reputation.

Its reputation as a hallucinogenic drink helped to elevate its status. Though there is no greater likelihood of this than with other strong liquors such as vodka or whisky. I have had a couple of bottles of absinthe over the years (or was it just one), but I have only recently discovered that I may not have been drinking it correctly. (From the bottle, in a brown paper bag, whilst sat on a park bench.) Apparently, the classic method of serving absinthe involves dripping water over and through a sugar cube into a stemmed glass of absinthe. During the process, it will turn cloudy and opaque (Louche).

In the 1990s, another method was created where the sugar was first soaked with alcohol and lit with a match. This created impressive entertainment but also distracted from the fact that a cheap fake absinthe will not louche. I think that the saying, "you win some, you louche some," was first uttered by Edward Munch, drunk on absinthe, shortly after completing his masterpiece, The Scream.

By the way, Wormwood Scrubs, the prison in London, lies close to the homonymous park (If you recall, 'of the same name'.) 'Scrubs' is short for scrubland, whilst wormwood, the herb, is commonly found on wasteland.

Head spinning, or was it the ceiling, and just before my eyes lost the battle with my eyelids and closed, I returned my thoughts to Phillip the Good, Son of John the Fearless (I'm now crying with hallucinogenic laughter.) his sympathies lay with the English, and the ties between England and Burgundy are fascinating. Trying to sniff out the bad in him, he had 24 mistresses and 18 illegitimate children; his forces were responsible for capturing Joan of Arc whom Phillip ransomed to the English. But Burgundy reached the pinnacle of its prestige during his reign, particularly known as a leading centre for the arts. Not really quite as bad as I would have enjoyed. I am always uncomfortable, though, with the phrase 'illegitimate children'; they are, after all, quite legitimately, children.

Day 61, 31st July, distance 77.48 kilometres + 16.07 kilometres (5,721.54 kilometres), elevation gain 1,501m + 168m (71,657m).

Depart: Pontarlier. Arrive: Damprichard.

Weather: Sunny, but cool mountain breeze 26.

Food: Fruit puree, yoghurt, baguette, cereal, breakfast biscuits, chicken baguette, croissant, and not just any old Calzone; this one was stuffed like a volcano, ready to erupt. (I know the feeling.)

Having believed we had left the mountains behind and never having cycled in this part of France, we find ourselves still in the Jura Mountains and among ski resorts! Ski resorts! I thought the Jura was the French equivalent of the Bannau Brycheiniog. (Formally the Brecon Beacons.)

We have a climb from the start out of Pontarlier, the Col de la Fresse. It's not challenging; in fact, the sort of climbs we fly up without panniers average less than 3% over 12 kilometres. Last night, absinthe could have jet-propelled us up if Kate had struck a match at the wrong time. (Possibly at the right time.)

After the descent and ascent, we pass through Les Gras, where streams running down the slopes of Mont-Chateleu form a beautiful waterfall, the Cascades des Chaudieres. Each section of the waterfall has worn the rock below with a swirl of pebbles in the current, gradually grinding into the rock underneath to create smooth bowl shapes. We follow the road 'round and up to the Grand Combe-Chateleu, before tracking the Doubs River and plunging down to Villers Le Lac, then parallel to the Swiss border (demarcated by the Doubs along here) to our destination. The dry weather today did nothing to lessen the plight of our destination, Damprichard (sometimes you do not need to make it up, but I usually do anyway!). We checked into our accommodation, and then headed into town to check out the restaurants and get provisions.

Not one single restaurant was open—two, at least, had chosen the same time to take a holiday, and another was open later in the week. So perhaps not for the last time, we headed for a shop, the Coccinelle Express (a shop rather than a fast beetle), but they had chosen today to do stock-taking. I can't help considering that a lack of communication and local planning exist in Damprichard; perhaps everyone owns a car. Half an hour later, we found ourselves in Maiche, having hopped back on the tandem. (Nice to find it so light for a change) and cycled the 8 kilometres to a shop and a pizza restaurant. (Which, of course, was well worth it.) I think we secretly both enjoyed the bonus ride, obsessed as we both may be.

Day 62, 1st August, distance 96.01 (5,817.55 kilometres), elevation gain 1,045m (72,702m).

Depart: Damprichard. Arrive: Delle.

Weather: Pluie-inondation. 17 degrees with horizontal needle rain in the face! (Pleasant evening, 22 degrees.)

Food: Pain au chocolates, madeleine, yoghurt, apple puree, bread rolls, sardines, gum chews, humus, that Greek aubergine thing a bit like lasagne, bulgur wheat, Citroen sorbet with rhum.

Torrential rain to start (Pluie—inondation). Richard is not the only one that's damp. We had a short pinch and a punch (first day of the month) climb to start today from Damprichard, just 3 kilometres away, averaging about 5% to the Col de La Vierge. The payback was about 7 kilometres downhill to the Swiss border and Le Doubs and then, unsurprisingly, a 7-kilometre climb from Goumois to Fessevillers (averaging just over 4%), and we still have torrential rain.

Our next climb came much later in the day, the Passage de la Douler, which starts from Saint-Hippolyte and climbs almost 10 kilometres via Chamesol, averaging about 5% with a few kicks of 6 or 7%, nothing too bad, finishing close to L'Escargot de la Ferme Du Lomont, still pluie-inondation.

The snail farm, at an altitude of 800 metres and close to Switzerland, can be visited from June to the end of September for a few euros, so it's not too much to shell out. Visits, though, are by appointment only, as the farmers eat and live there, and I believe they manage a gite there.

I get the impression we may be leaving the mountains. The climbs today really were relaxing, and the border with Switzerland must be running out soon. But the route was all over the place today, following the meandering borders and rivers. Some tempting short cuts were ignored!

Delle. Boy, where do you start? Delle is short for Deluge or it should be after the day we had. But it was a lovely place to finish in today, beautiful buildings, restaurants open, a delicious meal, no complaints, no worries. Kate can't believe how smoothly things are going and so decides to tempt fate, "I can't believe how smoothly things are going." (My powers of prediction astound even me; next she will probably start catastrophising.)

"I have a feeling that something is going to go wrong." (Great, let's hope that Kate's powers of prediction are less impressive than mine.)

Day 63, 2nd August, distance 128.21 kilometres (5,945.76 kilometres), elevation gain 776m (73,478m).

Depart: Delle. Arrive: Neuf-Brisach.

Weather: Dry, 28 degrees, wind occasionally very blustery, a few hearts in your mouth, moments.

Food: Pain au chocolate; yoghurt, fruit puree, Frosties bar, banana, pistachio tart, Chèvre and Miel pizza (wow).

The major European rivers are often wide and beautiful. They carve through countries, creating boundaries, and then break right through the countries, striking and meandering across them. They typically have fantastic cycle paths or quiet roads beside them that enable cyclists to comfortably cover hundreds of kilometres. The Rhine River begins in the Swiss Alps, and here, where we join it, it demarcates the border with Germany. It then flows in a mostly northerly direction through Germany and then in a westerly direction, carving its way across the Netherlands, where it reaches the North Sea between Rotterdam and Antwerp. It is the second-longest river in Central and Western Europe after the Danube, a section of which we have cycled from Passau to Vienna. I'd really recommend it. In order to work out where the Rhine meets the sea, I traced it across the map, and I was amazed with the places it passes through; Basel, Strasbourg, Cologne, Düsseldorf (my friend Rolf was born there), and Rotterdam, to mention a few.

The Rhine has been a vital navigable waterway, bringing trade and goods deep inland since the days of the Roman Empire. Unfortunately, the best cycle path is on the German side of the river, so we cycled mainly on what turned out to be a quiet but fast road. It had been a long while since we'd been on a long, flat road. We couldn't resist picking up the speed over the 40 kilometres or so!

As with many of our destinations, I was interested to see what today had in store. Neuf-Brisach is a fortified town that was founded in 1699 at the behest of Louis XIV. Looking at the map, it stands out in its symmetrical octagonal shape. Its parade ground, regimental roads, and octagonal shape, creating a citadel with fortified walls are nothing I have seen before. During the evening, after we had eaten out, we went for a walk around the town and also on parts of the walls.

"Have you seen anything like this before, Kate?"

"It does remind me of something I've seen on a map once."

Silent stare moment.

"That wouldn't be when I was plotting this route by any chance?" "Yes, it could have been."

Day 64, 3rd August, distance 86.37 kilometres (6,032.13 kilometres), elevation gain 116m (73,594m).

Depart: Neuf-Brisach. Arrive: Strasbourg.

Weather: Mainly dry, we were caught in a light shower, but not cold at 22 degrees.

Food: Cheese, bread, fruit puree, yoghurt, cheese sandwich, cereal biscuit, leaks, steak, vegetables, Madeleines soaked in rum.

An easy flat ride (okay, marginally downhill if you want to raise trivial objections) to Strasbourg today, similar to the second half of yesterday, mainly on a straight, flat quite quiet road with only the occasional opportunity to go next to the river.

I had hoped we could arrive here with a day in hand for a rest and a look around, and we did. Strasbourg is the official home of the European Parliament and, along with Brussels, Luxembourg, and Frankfurt, the fourth capital of the European Union. Many other important institutions are also based here. The city centre is on an apparent island, the Grande Île, and many parts of the city are picturesque and steeped in alcohol.

Arriving in Strasbourg takes us through industrial streets, but mainly on cycle paths over bridges and canals, finally arriving at the very grand Château de Pourtalès. It's an 18th-century chateau named after the Pourtalès family. It sounds and looks very grand, but in fact, has a mixed history. Originally a manor house, built around 1750, it was expanded into a chateau in about 1802. Various high-ranking owners lived in the chateau until the Franco-Prussian war, in 1870, when it suffered extensive damage in a fire. It continued to be the residence of the Pourtalès family until the First World War, when it was occupied by the Germans (not all of them), and then again in the Second World War. (No surprise, they had left excellent reviews on Trustpilot after their first visit.) It went through various guises, including as a hall of residence for absinthe-drinking university students.

In 2009, the Château de Pourtalès was converted into a hotel and has housed Members of the European Parliament before inviting and welcoming the absinthe-drinking Bosley family to stay.

We had a great, though long, walk into Strasbourg on the way, passing the European Court of Human Rights, the Council of Europe, and the L'Eglise Sant-Paul (built between 1890–1897) before arriving in the centre of Strasbourg with its mediaeval streets on the Grande Ile.

The Notre Dame Cathedral, built between 1180 and 1439, is over the top, Gothic grandeur. It is asymmetrical, with a 142-metre tower rising up from one side of the cathedral, which was the highest building in Europe until the 19th century. Its stunning stained-glass windows had to be removed and hidden from Hitler in salt mines during the Second World War. The rose window above the main entrance is particularly striking, and there is a remarkable astronomical clock built between 1571 and 1574.

Leaving the cathedral, we chose to walk along the canal to visit the area known as La Petite France. Unfortunately, the rain returned, and we took shelter underneath one of the bridges to watch the world go by for half an hour. We then found further refuge in a restaurant in La Petite, France, before taking a brief look around in the drizzle. Located at the western end of the Grand Île, La Petite France would be a delight to wander around on a fine day. Dating from the Middle Ages, this was once the city's industrial heart, home to its millers, tanners, and fishermen. It is here that you will find the largest concentration of Strasbourg's pastel-coloured, half-timbered buildings, dating from the 16th and 17th centuries.

Unfortunately, the weather was not going to improve, so we paid a very swift visit first to the Ponts Couverts, a set of four towers and three bridges dating from the mid-13th century. They were originally built as a defence for Strasbourg but were eventually superseded by the Barrage Vaudan over 400 years later. Their name comes from the wooden roof that originally covered the bridge, although the roof was torn down at the end of the 18th century. Then, right next to the Ponts Couverts, is the Barrage Vaudan, which is three things at once; a bridge, a weir and part of the city's defences built in the 17th Century. By now, we were getting a little damp, so we set off on the long walk back to the chateau for a shower before going out to eat. (Luckily, the rain had passed.)

This journey has been an unforgettable experience so far, and Strasbourg lived up to my expectations. I fear that the remaining days of our journey are going to be a disappointment as we head back towards Britain. Part of the journey will be next to Belgium for crying out loud!

Oh, and now another consequence of Brexit. Our mobile phone company had allowed us to use up to 5mb of our data whilst roaming in France, and we had been adding data every few weeks as we paid for 20mb and with it capped at 5mb, it kept running out. Now we can no longer do this and have no data allowance for the rest of the trip, so we have to rely on Wi-Fi. This is 2023; things really have gone backwards. Can we go back to the future please?

"We have got this far; what if something goes wrong now?" said Kate.

"It'll be better than if it had gone wrong 10 weeks ago." I said.

Day 65, 5th August, distance 131.56 kilometres (6,163.69 kilometres), elevation gain 819m (74,413m).

Depart: Strasbourg. Arrive: Bitche.

Weather: sunny spells, 22 degrees fine for cycling.

Food: Porridge, croissant, yoghurt, apricot, baguette, egg, cereal bar, breakfast biscuit, pate, toast, salmon, salad, chips.

Almost perfectly flat as we continue near the Rhine for about 70 kilometres, but not without a few U-turns and reroutes! The first came after following a really good piste for 10 kilometres or so; it then joined a tarmacked lane next to a canal until, after a couple of kilometres, there were some concrete blocks blocking the way. Beyond that, a canal crossed our path, and beyond that, on the other side of the canal, the road continued on. You are probably trying to picture that; it is as it says.

We then turned left (West) at the north-eastern corner of France, and still running along the border with Germany, we passed through Wissembourg and hit a climb, which is a shock to the legs but fun, over 5 kilometres with an average gradient of over 5% up the Col du Pigeonnier. At the top, there's a statue of a rambler, carved from wood, if I recall. It's a fun piece, a caricature of a walker with a rucksack and pots and pans hanging from his bag. A bit later, after the descent, we come across another statue, this time of a cyclist carrying his broken bicycle over his shoulder. It perfectly depicts what could be Eugene Christophe looking up forlornly with a bandaged knee.

The bike, though, is more recent, so it's not Christophe. As they say locally, and no doubt so would Christophe, "la vie est une salope," which I gather translates as, "Life's a Bitche," and that's understandable when, as an inhabitant of the area, you are known as Bitchois and Bitchoises (I was born in Manchester and I am therefore a Mancunian, fancy being called a Bitchois! Bitche is part of the Northern Vosges Regional Nature Park.)

A surprising place with a small population and being in a nature park, we were surprised to find a large fortress that had been built from a pre-existing castle at the beginning of the 13th century, dominating the skyline over the town. During the Franco-Prussian war, the citadel became known for its resistance when about 3,000 soldiers held on for 8 months against 20,000 enemy soldiers, only surrendering when ordered to do so as part of a ceasefire (1871.) The town actually became part of Germany until the end of the First World War. The hotel we stayed in felt as though it had also seen better days, though the room was perfectly reasonable. The restaurant, though, was very good and deservedly packed out.

Day 66, 6th August, distance 90.78 kilometres (6,254.47 kilometres), elevation gain 982m (75,395m).

Depart: Bitche. Arrive: Freyming.

Weather: Rain. 16 degrees. Wind 30–40kph gusts in exposed parts, which could be painful.

Food: Baguettes, jam, fruit, yoghurt, croissant, pain au raisin, pain au chocolate, peanuts, apple puree, big mac, potato wedges, side salad, chocolate cookie.

The French horn is a brass instrument that one that appears to curl around itself like a coil before the end of the tube splays open with an impressive, flared bell. That's what I was thinking of today as we cycled our first 8 or 9 kilometres beside the small river, La Horn, at dawn.

The weather was poor. Torrential rain from the outset. Kate and I are usually fair-weather cyclists, as I've mentioned before, but we will take it as it comes when we tour. It led to a discussion.

What would we do—sit in a hotel? We'd soon regret it, particularly if the weather turned out to be less than torrential rain with thunder and lightning. It might not be the best weather for cycling, but it's better than being bored; you have a sense of achievement when you get through it, and, hey, it's not usually so bad. In fact, it did improve—windy, but dry.

The destination is Freyming-Merlebach, not a long way, only 90 kilometres, but with the wind and the rain (did I mention the wind?) it did feel a bit longer.

The accommodation tonight is a cheap hotel, used mainly by workers or people passing through. Perfectly clean though, but no restaurant. The manager/receptionist is incredibly friendly and attentive. We had been told that we would need to keep the tandem in our room, but he had cleared a space in the linen room for us because he felt it would be too cramped. (It would have been.) When we had showered, we came to the entrance to walk to the nearest restaurant, and we stood at the door as another rain shower had just started. The manager walked out to his car and returned with an umbrella for us. How nice was that? (Well. It was really nice.) Unfortunately, we had one of those evenings when the only restaurant we could find was full. I've mentioned a number of times the difficulty we have had finding somewhere to eat. What you do tend to find, often in the smallest of towns, is a salon de coiffure—you may starve, but you'll have lovely hair for your funeral. What we did find was a McDonalds, which was better than nothing. (You can get a beer with your Big Mac in France!)

<u>Day 67</u>, 7th August, distance 104.34 kilometres (6,358.81 kilometres), elevation gain 1,425m (76,820m).

Depart: Freyming. Arrive: Thionville.

Weather: dry, about 17 degrees, but strong headwinds most of the day 20–35 kph.

Food: Croissants, baguettes, cereals, yoghurts, apple purees, pain au chocolate, croissants, fruit purée, seeded bread, charcuterie, tartiflette, baguettes.

The river Moselle flows down from the Vosges mountains and flows through this part of France, creating a natural border between Luxembourg and Western Germany at Schengen, where it ultimately joins the Rhine at Koblenz. Schengen is the location where the Schengen Agreement (1985) and the Schengen Convention (1990) were both signed to agree, shared responses to border controls. Since the Brexit decision, the UK now sits outside of the area, and one consequence is the requirement for us to have a visa if we stay within the area for more than 90 out of 180 days.

As we cycled down to the pretty village of Manderen, we could see a magnificent mediaeval castle on the hill overlooking the village. The castle was built between 1419 and 1434 and was originally called Mensburg castle and renamed Malbrouck castle in 1705 when John Churchill, Duke of Marlborough (called Malbrouck by the French) retreated his forces away from what would have been a significant conflict, leaving behind only his name for the castle. It was in ruins when it was bought by the General Council of the Moselle in 1975. Then substantial work began, and the castle was completely renovated from 1991 to 1998.

The castle of Malbrouck is very picturesque, with four towers, one at each corner connected by curtain walls, plus a three-storey main building and a vast central courtyard, creating a visually stunning chateau.

We were surprised to find another mediaeval site beside the Moselle, the Chateau des Ducs de Lorraine. The Château des Ducs de Lorraine is in Sierck-les-Bains, Moselle. This fortified castle is located on a rocky promontory and dominates the meandering Moselle at the point of the German, Luxembourg, and French borders.

Thionville is on the banks of the Moselle. It's a steel and mining city, but it also has an important architectural and historical legacy dating back to the Middle Ages. As we were based just outside the city, we only had a limited opportunity to see it. There is a marked walking circuit for investigating the city centre, including the Place du Marché featuring a belfry tower that contains what is known as the Great Bell of Thionville; there's a Neo-Classical Church, St Maximin, which holds a remarkable organ dating back to the 16th century; and also an archaeology museum in an 11th-century tower.

Day 68, 8th August, distance 86.73 kilometres (6,445.54 kilometres), elevation gain 1,356m (78,176m).

Depart: Thionville. Arrive: Marville.

Weather: Dry, 19 degrees, light wind.

Food: Croissants, pain au chocolate, baguette, cereal, apple puree, yoghurt, cheese, egg, cereal bar, breakfast biscuits, banana, quiche Lorraine, steak, frites.

The ride out of Thionville could have been on busy roads, but we were able to find some good cycle paths, and though for the best part of the first 10 kilometres, it was uphill, it was very pleasant. Unfortunately, until the last 20 kilometres it's difficult to recommend the route to anyone with nothing of much interest and lots of rundown and quite poor neighbourhoods. The cycling was perfectly safe, just uninspiring. About halfway, we arrived at Mont-Saint-Martin, just north of Longwy and probably a suburb of it, but my note didn't say what I was going to say about it.

Our stay is in the very old town of Marville, where, during the First World War, it was caught up in some fierce fighting, the Combat de Marville. In August 1914, the town was the scene of two battles. Initially, the charge of the 9th Cavalry Division on the 10th of August then, on the 25th of August, the battle was fought by the 7th Infantry Division. An interesting detail from the first battle describes where the 24th Dragoon regiment was sent to attack the woods whilst the group of cyclist hunters attacked the edge from the west. We were lucky enough to be able to store our tandem in a locked garage, safe from any local cyclist hunters.

I just went to the kitchen to grab a sandwich, and having returned, immediately recalled why I was going to mention Mont-Saint-Martin; we were at the borders of Luxembourg and Belgium, and knew that we were truly heading home. What's that about? You come in a room and forget something; you go out, and when you come back, you suddenly remember it?

"Typical, I've gone back into the kitchen and now I can remember what it was!" I said.

"Oh good, what was it?" Kate replied.

Me:

Day 69, 9th August, distance 78.68 kilometres (6,524.22 kilometres), elevation gain 1,131m (79,307m).

Depart: Marville. Arrive: Vrigne-Aux-Bois.

Weather: 21 degrees, sunny spells, occasional shower, sunny by 4 p.m.

Food: Croissants, baguettes, cereals, bread, cakes, eggs, plums, sweets, breakfast biscuits, peanuts, goat's cheese salad, Chèvre, and Miel pizza.

It was wet again and a bit cool to start with, but we had the feeling straight away that today was going to be a great ride. Despite Kate's worries, we have continued to escape injury and illness, and now, into our last week of the tour, having done over 6,500 kilometres, we have relaxed a lot and often pushed a little harder, even on some climbs. Quite soon into the ride, we came to Montmedy and immediately began a short 2-kilometre climb, the Cote de la Citadelle, up to the Citadelle overlooking the town. The Citadelle was built on the sight of a previous castle by order of Charles V, around 1545 and was within Luxembourg, which in turn was then part of the Netherlands.

It became a part of France in 1659 as part of the Treaty of the Pyrenees. The entrance to the Citadelle is impressive and can be cycled through (it remains inhabited), crossing a couple of bridges, through an archway, and then, a tunnel with a traffic light system as it is very narrow. Once you emerge from the tunnel into the Citadelle, you are now on cobbled roads with old buildings, some of which are derelict, and on your left, an impressive church. During the French Revolution in 1791, the fortress was believed to be the destination of King Louis XVI and his family in their attempt to escape from the burgeoning anti-monarchy radicalisation in the capital, Paris. The area at the time was overwhelmingly pro-monarchy. The king, though, never arrived because they were discovered en route and escorted back to the capital city.

Cycling back out of the Citadelle, we had a gradual but fast descent down a smooth road alongside the valley over the hill from Montmardy, through which the Thonne river was flowing. To our left below, we could see where a railway line had reappeared from its exit through a tunnel from Montmardy and was curving over a beautiful viaduct beside the village of Thonne-les-Pres.

The weather was still variable, but we were passing through delightful villages, and we were lucky enough to arrive in a farming village just as the clouds burst, and there we found a shelter with a bench where we could have our lunch. For about 15 minutes, it poured, and rain was gushing down the street and overflowing the gutters, but once we had eaten, it stopped as quickly as it had started, the sun emerged, and the roads began to steam as the water evaporated from the surface.

Vrigne-aux-Bois was only recently created out of a merger of the town with a small village in 2017 called Bosseval-et-Briancourt. It is very close to the border with Belgium. A small forge was established in the area during the 16th century, but otherwise the area remained very quiet until the beginning of the 19th century. In 1822, Jean-Nicolas Gendarme created a metalwork factory with a blast furnace running on coal. A chateau was built for Monsieur Gendarme, and the town grew into what it is today.

Apparently, Sedan, just a few kilometres south-east, has a particularly impressive castle that is the largest fortress in Europe, I believe, but we didn't go there; hopefully another time.

Day 70, 10th August, distance 115.87 kilometres (6,640.09 kilometres), elevation gain 1,231m (80,538m).

Depart: Vrigne. Arrive: Les Grands Riaux.

Weather: Sunny 30 degrees by early afternoon, and glorious.

Food: Croissants, rice pudding, bread, honey, bananas, ham and cheese sandwiches, cereal biscuits, bananas, cured meats, and cheese sandwiches, yoghurt, fruit, peanuts, chocolate.

Again, we could tell immediately that today was going to be another great cycling day. The start of today's ride (which is through the Ardennes) runs parallel to the Meuse River, which grows in size and beauty each time we see a glimpse of it. After about 20 kilometres of wonderful cycling, we turn away from the river and head north-east up the Col de Loup, a 7.3-kilometre-long climb with a comfortable average gradient of 3.6%. The views of the hills and valleys of the Ardennes on the way up are magnificent. The Meuse meanders through one valley after another, and you can see one hillside after another overlapping each other like a childish drawing of hills (in fact, about my standard)—beautifully simple yet stunning.

We then coast down to a tributary of the Meuse, the Semois. Crossing a picturesque bridge over to the opposite bank of the Semois provides beautiful views of the villages and the river as we cycle along the cycle route that we meander along. We ride beside the river until re-joining the Meuse down curvaceous and scenic valleys up to the border with Belgium. We now had a 10-kilometre climb from Fumay up to Maison Brûlée (averaging 3% with some short kicks up to 7%.) The sun is out, about 30 degrees, so it feels harder than it should be, but cycling by the rivers on the Vieu Verte trans-Ardennes cycle route has been fun, picturesque, and easy, so we have no complaints. We'll have to come back, perhaps with family, because the cycle path is great.

Today we stayed in an apartment with no shops or restaurants nearby, so we planned to eat in Fumay at lunchtime. but after looking for somewhere in the heat, we had to make do with a sandwich and what we had left to drink. We thought we would find a shop near our destination, but the nearest place appeared to be 8 kilometres away. We were going to have to do a ride to the shop but decided to get to our stay and unpack the tandem for a faster ride. (If you are forced to ride, you may as well enjoy it!) The accommodation was literally next to the border on a quiet road that only passed between Belgium and France at the edge of the Ardennes, and we arrived at the lodgings with no food or drink.

Although we were very early, the host welcomed us and whilst walking through their beautiful garden, reminded us that breakfast is included. (That's a bonus, one thing we don't have to shop for.) She then shows us the lovely accommodation, which is comfortable and spacious and includes a fridge, but when she opens it, our mouths drop open. It's a full fridge; our fridge at home is never so full. It's a 'Bilbo Baggins' of a fridge that could cater to an unexpected party. Sometimes things just sort themselves out, don't they? No extra bike rides, just rest and relaxation on a glorious evening on a patio in the sun.

Day 71, 11th August, distance 80.61 kilometres (6,720.70 kilometres), elevation gain 766m (81,304m).

Depart: Les Grands Riaux. Arrive: Mairieux.

Weather: 28 degrees, Glorious sunny day, light breeze, no hint of rain.

Food: Croissants, yoghurt, pain au chocolate, banana, ham and cheese baguette, peanuts, croissants, pate, sausage, pork steak in cheese sauce (doesn't work for me!), crème brûlée.

Breakfast was also plentiful and delicious here, including a basket of fresh croissants, baguettes, pain au chocolates, pastries (presumably, purchased from quite a long way away). We were good to go again and head off through the nearby Foret Domaniale de Saint Michel. Cycling through the forest was an adventure in itself with rabbits, squirrels, and mice scurrying off as we approached. Up ahead, we could see deer on the track, but they were always aware of us approaching and casually bound away into the woods. Plotting a path through the woods hadn't been easy. Trying to decide which routes were paved, which were gravel, or which were grass or mud, and we had to make a couple of route changes, including when we came across another track for military use only, but these were only minor, and cycling here at this time in the morning was exciting.

Even after this slow but enjoyable start, the day was reasonably fast, with pleasant rolling hills on good, quiet roads, never needing to drop into a lower set of gears and passing even more beautiful villages. At one point, a large reddish bird of prey, possibly a red kite, was sitting at the roadside. It appeared very relaxed, almost confident, as it took off just in front of us, casually flying across our path, and then next to us, with us for 50 metres or more.

The red kite is a large bird of prey that has a pale grey head with dark streaks, a yellow beak with a dark hook, and pale eyes. Its angled, red wings are black-tipped and have white patches underneath it and it has a long, distinctive, reddish-brown, forked tail that sends it soaring up through the atmosphere, up where the air is clear.

The only disappointment of the day was the location of our destination. We arrived by 1 p.m., but there was really nothing to do, until the evening meal. We went for a walk, but much of it was beside a main road, nowhere to get a drink, and no sights to see. The 4-course evening meal made up for it, though!

Day 72, 12th August, distance 80.87 kilometres (6,801.57 kilometres), elevation gain (81,773m).

Depart: Mairieux. Arrive: Roeux.

Weather: Rain am 19 degrees; Sunny pm 30 degrees.

Food: Croissants, yoghurt, fruit puree, baguette, egg, lamb, potatoes, vegetables, tarte au pomme.

Unfortunately, we left Mairieux in the rain, or did we leave Mairieux whilst it was raining? After all, maybe the rain followed us, and the sun came out once we had left. Either way, it was difficult to see the route on the Garmin computer. We had about 2 hours of rain whilst we wrapped up and just got on with it. Conditions then changed quite quickly, and we had more sun than clouds, which made it very pleasant. We stopped for some lunch at an 'Artisanal Épicerie' where they always have excellent local produce for sale, but perhaps never what you really want at that moment in time. The owner took our order for coffee, but when asked for food, endeavoured to explain that the only thing she had was Tarte de Fromage, Flemish. (Or did she say Flamiche.)

She could tell we were a bit unsure, and her English was limited, so she went in and returned with a large cheese tart, which looked amazing, though rather filling. I thought I could comfortably eat half of it, but Kate's appetite was not up to eating the other half. We decided that we would have it, eat half of it between us, and save the rest for tomorrow's lunch. Pleased with our decision, the lady went in to prepare our food and drink. She did come out, though, to clarify how we wanted the tart, hot or cold. That was perfect; we asked for hot for me and cold for Kate (50/50) so that we could then share the hot half and keep the cold half for tomorrow, which would have been complicated to explain.

At this point, we'd fallen into the belief that she understood what we were saying, and we understood what she was saying. Subsequently, out came our order, one very large, heavily loaded, and hot cheese tart, with my coffee (hot milk) and Kate's coffee (cold milk). I have to say, I had no regrets that I was able to eat ¾ of that incredible tart! I subsequently looked up Flemish cheese tarts and discovered that 'Flamiche' is a savoury pastry, and the name means Flemish cake, so that may well be what the lady was calling it.

We came across something today that was both a shock and also very exciting. We should have been thinking about it, but we had overlooked our increasing proximity to Roubaix. We turned a corner and juddered to a halt. Pavés, the French word for cobblestones. Cobblestoned roads were the norm over 100 years ago, and today they live on in many classic cycling races such as Paris-Roubaix. Kate said I was grinning ear to ear, and I knew I was feeling very pleased to have arrived. This was a reasonably nice, uniform, and clean section, and though a heavily loaded road tandem is not specifically designed for this, we cautiously and steadily cycled along it so as not to follow in the footsteps of Eugene Christophe. Magical. It wasn't to be the only section; the next piece was rougher, less uniform, and a bit gappy, but safely traversed and enjoyed. (Don't ask why; I have no idea.)

Our destination, a small rural village called Roeux, was located adjacent to the border with Belgium. Once showered and clothes washed, we had a pleasant 3-kilometre walk into town, across fields to shop, and for a meal to eat. It should have been an enjoyable return walk, but I began to feel unusually uncomfortable in my 'aqua' shoes, and with about 1 kilometre to go, my right knee gave way. Suddenly. I had to stop, slowly stretching my leg, then hobbling back. I hadn't seen this coming, no warnings, no aches, or pains. I had the pain all evening and through the night, and I kept trying to slowly stretch and massage my leg.

It even continued the following morning with me struggling down the stairs.

"How many days do we have to go?"

Kate replied that we had three.

"I'm sure that'll be fine; you may be pedalling whilst I put my feet up!"

That wasn't a joke, and Kate had done it before; we were on a tour from the north of England to the south coast and had about 120 kilometres to go of a long 145-kilometre ride when our front bottom bracket broke. Kate had to cycle the rest of the journey that day whilst I tried to find somewhere to rest my feet that didn't result in cramps or pins and needles! When you tell people about that, the initial response is incredulity that Kate would be able to do that. Of course, it is incredible; Kate doesn't give up that easily. But there is also a lot more to it. I still have control of the gears, but no longer any pedalling resistance that tells me when I need to change gear on Kate's behalf; I'm sat with all my weight on the bike with no relief from the action of pedalling to relieve the pressure and impact off my bum; I have no step down (a pedal) when we come to a stop at a junction, increasing the likelihood that we could just topple over. Things could get worse then, but we'll be fine.

Day 73, 13th August, distance 102.80 kilometres (6,904.37 kilometres), elevation gain 385m (82,158m).

Depart: Roeux. Arrive: Saint-Jans-Cappel.

Weather: Cloudy, but dry, 24 degrees, that'll do; may have to take some layers off.

Food: Bananas, yoghurt, fruit cocktail, baguette, sardines, breakfast biscuits, cheese tart, fish and vegetable stew, chocolate birthday cake.

For the past couple of days, it has been noticeable that many of the houses, farms, and even churches are built with distinctive red brick with white, or very light-coloured, mortar. I have heard the term 'flemish bond' and assume these are examples of that; in any case, it is distinctive.

My leg is working reasonably well on the bike. It's probably able to cope with the demands of cycling even though something is damaged. It does feel weak, and it is a bit of a struggle to uncleat it must be time to finish the tour!

Having cycled on some cobbled sections yesterday, I suggested that I have no idea why I enjoyed it, but I probably do know why, and it relates to their historic cycling significance. Today we found ourselves on some sections of the route of the Hell of the North, passing sections of pavés at Camphin-en-Pevele and Willems, but not on the cobbles. (That came unexpectedly early yesterday.) The Hell of the North or Paris-Roubaix is one of the greatest races in cycling and, established in 1896, one of the oldest. It's a tough, rough, and technical challenge, with many cobbled sections on the route that need to be overcome. Some of these are unforgiving, dangerous, and, of course, hellish. The name 'Hell of the North', came from a group of race officials who, after inspecting the route after the First World War, described its condition as 'hell'.

After the Second World War, the roads were significantly improved, but this created a dilemma for Paris-Roubaix as it could lose its almost mythical status as the Hell of the North. No worries though; the organisers located the remaining cobbled and rutted road sections and created a route that used many of them, thus retaining its character. To this day, the race retains gladiatorial status. It was not until 2021 that the first women's edition of the race took place. The winner was a British rider, Lizzie Deignan, who attacked the leaders from about 80 kilometres from the finish, going on to win the race with a stunning solo ride worthy of the renowned nature of the event.

Whilst cycling through Roubaix, we passed the Parc du Lion. We both recognised the name but couldn't recall having visited it, so we can only assume it is well known. The Parc du Lion is a large green space located in the heart of Wattrelos, France. It offers a variety of outdoor and sporting activities for visitors. The park also has a Farm 'Pedagogique', where visitors can learn about traditional farming practices and interact with farm animals.

Nearing our destination today, we cycled through the town of Bailleul, which was several times destroyed during its history it was rebuilt after the First World War. The main square, with typical Flemish architecture, is full of charm, with its beautiful houses and its town hall with an imposing 62-metre-high bell tower. (Seemingly built in competition with the nearby church.) There is also the most garish Chateau d'eau that I have seen, built facing the church and the town hall. It is white and has what looks like a large, fortified entrance! I asked our hosts that evening about it, and they said it's the headquarters of the area's wastewater and sewage treatment company. "Well, where there's muck there's brass."

We spent the evening with our French hosts and two other guests, and it was a very social occasion with an opportunity to learn about some local culture and traditions. The two highlights for me were throwing metal discs at frogs and waterboarding the other male guest to celebrate his birthday. (The chateau d'eau had just been a warning of things to come.)

Perhaps both activities need a little more explanation. We were introduced to a French frog game, Jeux de la Grenouille. The frog game is a shuffleboard-style game present in many European countries. It is in the form of a box or barrel with holes on the upper part, the central hole being a frog with its mouth open. Players stand about 3 metres from the box and try to get the most points by throwing cast-iron discs and aiming to get them down the open holes. Different holes have different point values, and, of course, the hole yielding the most points is the mouth of the frog. I have to say, I seemed to be playing quite well (beginner's luck) until our host managed to get his puck in the frog's mouth—we all agreed that was the winning shot.

We also had a cake during the evening to celebrate the birthday of one of the guests. This was followed by what appeared to be subjecting him to waterboarding—presumably to get him to admit his age. I must confess (he didn't) that I have failed to find out what this was all about. They sang what they said was a traditional anniversary song and, whilst doing so, held a cloth over his head whilst dripping water through it. Kate and I decided it was time for bed, as we had some cycling to do tomorrow, and I was carrying an injury! "Pour le prochain match, nous nous déshabillons…"

Day 74, 14th August, distance 74.62 kilometres (6,978.99 kilometres), elevation gain 325m (82,483m).

Depart: Saint-Jans-Cappel. Arrive: Dunkerque.

Weather: Sunny 31 degrees, put on plenty of sun cream if you are naked.

Food: Read, croissants, yoghurt, peanuts, charcuterie, tandoori chicken, pakora, chicken madras, rice, plain nan, kulfi.

It's a beautiful day today, and it looks like my knee is going to hold out. No pain whilst pedalling, but still painful and weak when I have to uncleat and it stiffens up when I sit, still making it difficult to walk. Today we passed the northernmost part of our journey, Bray-Dunes. Bray-Dunes is situated on the Belgian border, at the most northerly point of mainland France. During the Dunkerque evacuation in WW2, it was the site of many fatalities. We tend to focus on the incredible achievement of the evacuation of the troops from

Dunkerque, which was unusual as it felt like a victory (and an important morale boost) when in reality it was a retreat and a defeat. But we shouldn't forget the lives lost and those severely wounded. Over a little more than a month, the British Expeditionary Force suffered 68,000 casualties, including 3,500 killed.

Dunkerque is a seaside town with miles of sandy beaches, dunes, and acres of protected parkland. The French coast of Flanders is known for its kite surfing, sand-yachting, cycling, and hiking. Museums offer opportunities to uncover the past, including the Battle of Dunkerque museum, which houses a collection of wartime relics and moving images; the Operation Dynamo Museum; a number of memorials, including the British Memorial; the Fort des Dunes, and the memorial to the battles of May and June 1940, all located within easy walking distance, and pay tribute to all those that fought at Dunkerque.

We have now almost reached the end of our tour, and it's the middle of the summer holidays. The seafront was very crowded, including restaurants, so we decided to stroll a few streets back and found ourselves in an Indian restaurant for a great meal.

Getting back home after an adventure: 15th August, distance 22.74 kilometres + 74.36 kilometres (7,001.73 kilometres in France), elevation gain 43m + 852m (82,526m elevation gain 'round France.)

Depart: Dunkerque. Arrive: Maidstone.

Weather: Sunny spells, 26 degrees, a bit breezy on the coast.

Food: Croissants, baguettes, yoghurts, chicken sandwiches, pastries, packets of crisps, macaroons, tacos, salads, beans.

The route from Dunkerque to Loon-Plage was flat and easy, mainly on cycle paths of just over 20 kilometres. Once comfortably on board in our stockinged feet, we enjoyed a celebratory Prosecco on the DFDS ferry in the premium lounge as we relaxed on the journey. A nice treat and very relaxing. 'Stockinged feet'; we have such a weird language! Let's not pay too much attention to the cycle shoe policy, which results in us being in our stockinged feet as it's deemed safer than our mountain bike shoes. (With the embedded cleats, they are no different from hiking boots, of course.)

From the ferry, we cycled about 10 kilometres to the Battle of Britain Memorial at Capel-Le-Ferne (honest, we are in England!) to meet Kate's parents for a coffee. The route from Dover to the memorial is almost totally on a good cycle path. The site provides a tribute to those who defeated the Luftwaffe in the Battle of Britain in 1940. The clifftop memorial has replica Spitfire and hurricane planes, a memorial wall and a visitor's centre, 'The Wing' which is a modern interactive museum with a decent cafe. We then undertook the remaining journey home cycling at quite some speed, as though to burn off any excess energy that we hadn't used over the previous 12 weeks!

As we cycled home from Dover, a vision entered my head that as we approached our streets, there would be streams of people walking away from our house carrying furniture and belongings identical to those we own, and as we drew up outside our house, a small Hobbit was standing on a plinth auctioning off our belongings. The plinth stood next to a couple of shallow graves with a large iron ball in front, half buried in the lawn, being used as a headstone.

"And how can you prove you are the deceased, Mr Bosley?"

"I've got my Brexit passport. How did you get in my house? On second thoughts, don't answer that," I respond, looking down at the overturned doormat and glancing back at the inconveniently situated graves blocking my driveway, "and I'm not deceased!"

Will We Do Something Similar in the Future?

The answer to this question could provide an insight into how much we enjoyed the tour. Describing what the experience of cycling 'round a country is like is quite difficult to do. The story itself gives a feel for that. The variety of things we have seen, often just in one day, shows how wonderful being able to tour on a bike can be. Kate always says that cycling is slow enough to be able to get a good look at what is around you, see things you wouldn't otherwise see, go to places you wouldn't otherwise go, or go to them on a route you wouldn't otherwise take, seeing them in a different way and getting to really know a country and its people. It gives you the opportunity to see what differences there are between us and other people, but actually, much more so, what the similarities are and how friendly people can be.

Touring without the support of a backup vehicle carrying your gear also brings its own challenges and rewards; deciding what you really need to take or, harder, what you don't need to take. That in itself provides some life lessons about survival, about self-consciousness, and about what really matters rather than what is unnecessary. Even though we weren't camping, people were surprised at how little we were carrying. (Whilst we still carried things, we didn't need.) The way we planned our trip was successful. We got to where we wanted to be, we saw what we wanted, we survived physically very comfortably, and we had what we needed. We wouldn't do everything exactly the same, though. Not because we could 'improve' things, carry slightly less, ride further each day, and so on, but to experience things differently, take tiny steps out of our comfort zone, and see things from the perspectives of others.

Will we do a similar cycle again? Well, what do you think? We can't wait. Kate has said that the length (in time) of this one was just about right, so I already have something to work towards. A tour that is no more than about 12 weeks long, hmmm, how much planning shall I do this time?

Writing the Book

I have always wanted to write a book and felt the best opportunity for this would be when I retired, which I have (December 2021). Of course, that also gives me the time to plan and ride a significant tour—something that both Kate and I have wanted to do. (And Kate, since her accident in 2013, has had to patiently wait for me to retire.)

The reason for writing a book is just for enjoyment—the fun of just putting 'pen to paper' whilst providing a purposeful activity to ease into retirement and create a record of the ride.

"Write it down before we forget it all," Kate said.

That puzzled me.

"What is there to forget?"

"About what?" she replied.

The potential for publication would depend on the quality of that record and, of course, the interest in that written record by a publisher. The latter is not within my control, of course, but I had no unrealistic expectations for this book and no desperate need for that outcome, other than that it would be a nice bonus. I could, however, put in some reasonable effort to create an interesting record. I scribbled some quick thoughts about what the book could include:

- A record tour of interest to cyclists, walkers, and perhaps holiday makers.
- Places of interest. (Of interest to walkers, holiday makers and cyclists.)
- How to plan for a tandem tour? (Of interest to cyclists.)
- Funny. (Of interest to most that have at least some sense of humour)
- How to train for a multi-day tour? (Of interest to cyclists.)
- Pictures of food. (Who doesn't like that?)

I also decided to set up a Facebook page, Snails around France, thinking this would enable me to interact with other touring cyclists and tandem riders and perhaps learn from them. Writing this book has been a joy and never a chore.

But I owe a great deal of thanks to Kate for allowing me to do it whilst she has continued with more than a fair share of household chores and at times entertaining herself with the pointless, mind-numbing pastime of completing jigsaws. She deserves another tandem tour, as soon as possible.

Bibliography

Recycling Me: Back on the Bike by Kate Bosley

One Man and His Bike: A Life-Changing Journey All the Way Around the Coast of Britain by Mike Carter

Eat Sleep Cycle: A Bike Ride Around the Coast of Britain by Anna Hughes

The Mental Cyclist by Kyle Macrae

It's Too Late Now by A. A. Milne

Over the Alps on a Bicycle by Elizabeth Robins Pennell

San Fairy Ann Cycling Club: A Century of Cycling by Lise Taylor-Vebel

100 Greatest Hill Climbs by Simon Warren

Wheels of Chance by H. G. Wells